CONNECTING THE DOTS

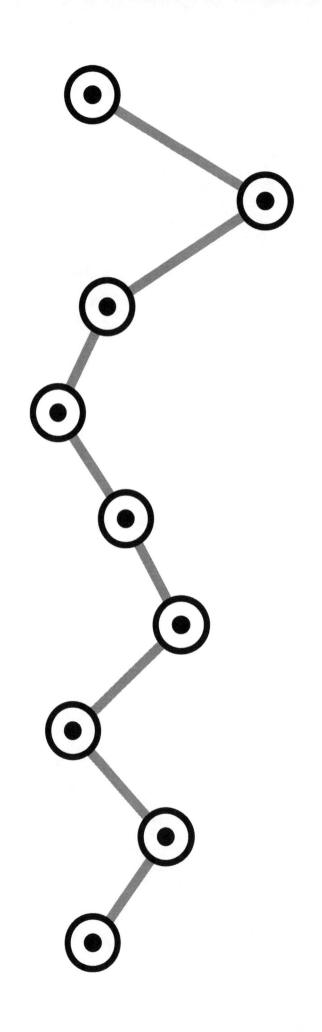

CONNECTING THE DOTS

Developing Student Learning Outcomes and Outcomes-Based Assessments

Second Edition

Ronald S. Carriveau

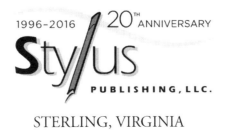

1996–2016 20TH ANNIVERSARY

Stylus
PUBLISHING, LLC.

STERLING, VIRGINIA

Published by Stylus Publishing, LLC
22883 Quicksilver Drive
Sterling, Virginia 20166-2102

Library of Congress Cataloging-in-Publication Data
Names: Carriveau, Ronald S., author.
Title: Connecting the dots : developing student
learning outcomes and outcomes-based assessments /
Ronald S. Carriveau.
Description: Second edition. |
Sterling, Virginia : Stylus Publishing, LLC, [2016] |
Includes bibliographical references and index.
Identifiers: LCCN 2016014463 (print) |
LCCN 2016024088 (ebook) |
  ISBN 9781620364796 (cloth : alk. paper) |
  ISBN 9781620364802 (pbk. : alk. paper) |
  ISBN 9781620364819
  (library networkable e-edition) |
  ISBN 9781620364826 (consumer e-edition)
Subjects: LCSH: Educational evaluation. |
Academic achievement--Evaluation. |
Educational tests and measurements. |
Education, Higher.
Classification: LCC LB3051 .C366 2016 (print) |
LCC LB3051 (ebook) | DDC 379.1/58--dc23
LC record available at https://lccn.loc.gov/2016014463

13-digit ISBN: 978-1-62036-479-6 (cloth)
13-digit ISBN: 978-1-62036-480-2 (paperback)
13-digit ISBN: 978-1-62036-481-9 (library
networkable e-edition)
13-digit ISBN: 978-1-62036-482-6 (consumer
e-edition)

Printed in the United States of America

All first editions printed on acid-free paper
that meets the American National Standards Institute
Z39-48 Standard.

Bulk Purchases

Quantity discounts are available for use in
workshops and for staff development.
Call 1-800-232-0223

First Edition, 2016

10 9 8 7 6 5 4 3 2

Validity matters.

Thomas M. Haladyna

Contents

PREFACE   *ix*

ACKNOWLEDGMENTS   *xi*

INTRODUCTION   *1*

1. DEVELOPING STUDENT LEARNING OUTCOMES   *3*

2. TEMPLATES FOR WRITING TEST QUESTIONS   *17*

3. DEVELOPING AN OVERALL ASSESSMENT PLAN AND TEST BLUEPRINT   *27*

4. WRITING MULTIPLE-CHOICE TEST ITEMS   *37*

5. WRITING CONSTRUCTED-RESPONSE ITEMS   *47*

6. WRITING AND USING SCORING RUBRICS   *51*

7. MEASURING CRITICAL THINKING WITH MULTIPLE-CHOICE ITEMS   *57*

8. REPORTING RESULTS WITH THE THREE-LEVEL MODEL   *69*

9. APPLYING THE THREE-LEVEL MODEL AT THE INSTITUTIONAL LEVEL AND BEYOND   *85*

REFERENCES   *97*

INDEX   *99*

Preface

There is a need in the education process for clear communications with students about what they are expected to know and do, how they are achieving and have achieved, and how to communicate results to stakeholders. The purpose of this book is to address these needs. It is written for teachers, staff, and administrators at all levels and can be used as a reference or a textbook. It offers an organized and effective way to develop quantifiable outcomes, measure them, and communicate student learning achievement of the outcomes at the course and institutional levels and beyond. The outcome-based model in this book provides the structure that is needed to effectively communicate with all stakeholders, from students to teachers and administrators to educational and governing organizations.

Every day in every classroom at every level of education, students and teachers interact either in a face-to-face or online environment. We assume that a major topic in their communication is about learning expectations and assessment. Yet, I have asked my students many times, particularly at the postsecondary levels, about their learning experiences, and it was not uncommon to hear students say that specific learning expectations were not made clear to them; that expectations were not addressed in the instruction, that assessments didn't match what was taught, and that test items were unfair.

When I have asked teachers if I could see their specific learning outcomes and the links between their outcome statements and their test items, I have typically found little evidence of a clear connection. When I asked what evidence they had that their learning outcomes, instruction, and assessment were aligned and whether their instructional implementation was effective, many faculty admitted to a lack of alignment and effectiveness evidence. When I see what evidence of learning is communicated at the institutional levels, there is typically not a clear link between course-level outcome attainment and institutional expectations. The dots are not connected.

This is not to say that teachers don't address to varying degrees alignment of learning outcomes, instruction, assessment, and reporting. Teachers usually can provide, at least in broad terms, what they are going to teach and what students are expected to learn. Teachers also know that some type of measurement is needed in order to determine the degree to which students are learning and have learned, but they typically don't tie assessment items directly to specific student learning outcome statements. Teachers and institutions are interested in the effectiveness of their instruction based on how well students performed on assessments, and institutions want evidence of student learning to be reported in a way that can be used to report to various governing organizations. This book provides the organizational structure needed to connect the dots among instruction, high-quality outcomes, high-quality outcome-based assessment, and meaningful reporting.

The first edition of *Connecting the Dots* has been used by many educators and institutions, nationally and internationally, and is the basis for the NextGen Course Redesign Program at the University of North Texas (UNT) that originally served as the Quality Enhancement Plan (QEP) for the Southern Association of Colleges and Schools' (SACS) accreditation requirement. The NextGen QEP program received exemplary status by SACS and was recommended as a model to be shared with other institutions. The NextGen program is managed by the Center for Learning Enhancement, Assessment, and Redesign at UNT.

This second edition of *Connecting the Dots* provides enhancements and additional examples and adds one entirely new chapter.

Chapter 1 provides step-by-step procedures for developing student learning outcome statements and introduces the three-level model.

Chapter 2 provides several templates for writing test questions. The templates are also useful for developing outcome statements.

Chapter 3 provides what is always needed when beginning an outcome-based assessment project—an assessment plan.

Chapter 4 provides what you need to know about constructing high-quality multiple-choice (selected-response) items.

Chapter 5 provides what you need to know about construction of high-quality constructed-response items.

Chapter 6 shows how to write and use outcome-based scoring rubrics.

Chapter 7 addresses the measurement of critical thinking, a necessary skill when solving problems.

Chapter 8 explains item-analysis statistics for selected-response and constructed-response assessment and their role in reporting results across levels with the three-level model.

Chapter 9 is new and provides a census approach for mapping outcome attainment from the course level to the institutional level and beyond.

Acknowledgments

For this second edition I thank again those faculty members I recognized in the first edition for their creative thoughts and the use of their course materials: Nicole Dash, Brenda McCoy, Elizabeth Turner, and Tracey Gau. Continued special acknowledgement to my friend and mentor Thomas M. Haladyna for his wonderful books (Haladyna 1997, 1999) on the construction of selected-response items and guidelines for writing multiple-choice items, used as a primary source for Chapter 4. Continued acknowledgment to Steven J. Osterlind (Osterlind, 1998) and Robert L. Linn and Norman E. Groulund for their books (Linn & Groulund, 1995, 2000) on the construction of outcomes and item development, which were used as sources for chapters 4 and 5. Thanks to my loving wife, Theresa, for her editing reviews and recommendations. Thanks to Adam Blake, graduate student, for converting the many tables and figures in the book to images for publishing. A special acknowledgment to Mike Simmons, an executive director at the University of North Texas and education consultant, for his input on the development of the second edition and especially for his recommendation for a census approach for the three-level model.

Introduction

Demands for quality at all levels of education are higher than they have ever been. Research in education, curriculum, assessment, and measurement is abundant. There is pressure on teachers to improve the quality of their instruction and to increase student learning. Making clear what students must learn, setting standards, measuring how well students learn, and redesigning instruction to create a more engaging and productive learning environment are being stressed by federal and state governments and by professional and national accreditation organizations at all levels. Faculty need outcome-based information for formative and summative assessment purposes. Institutions expect course-level outcomes to be mapped to program and institutional Goals and outcome attainment and to be reported in a way that satisfies accreditors and education boards.

The call for competency measures and individualized instruction is on the rise. Awarding credit for prior learning experience is on the rise. The Association of American Colleges & Universities' (AAC&U) Liberal Education and America's Promise (LEAP) Essential Learning Outcomes assessed by their Valid Assessment of Learning in Undergraduate Education (VALUE) rubrics, the Lumina Foundation's Degree Qualifications Profile's (DQP) five categories of learning outcomes, Tuning USA's discipline learning outcomes, and the role of outcome attainment in a competency model are now part of the national focus.

This book is about how teachers and institutions can meet these demands by obtaining, managing, using, and reporting valid outcome attainment measures at the course level and mapping outcome attainment from the course level to department, degree program, and institutional levels and beyond. It is about communicating clearly what students are expected to know and be able to do; developing assessments that measure the expectations; and producing test scores that are valid for their intended use and interpretation so that valid inferences can be made about students, courses, and programs. It is about optimizing course-level results by using a census approach in which all student responses are used for calculating the attainment values, which are then mapped to program and institutional levels, thus reducing or eliminating the need for sampling artifacts that are embedded in courses. It is a how-to manual that will guide you through the steps for developing measurable Student Learning Outcomes (SLOs) and assessments that measure the SLOs. It is rich with guidelines, forms, and examples to help achieve these goals.

Best practices and guidelines for developing test items and assessments are provided so that measurement error can be minimized. When error is not minimized, incorrect levels of achievement or performance may be inferred, and judgments made about students, courses, and programs may be inaccurate. The outcomes and assessment development guidelines in this book can be applied to the three primary domains for which learning outcomes and assessments are developed:

1. **Cognitive Domain.** This domain includes knowledge, skills, and intellectual abilities. The knowledge category covers a range of cognitive tasks from simple to complex. The skills category can include performance skills such as using a computer program or certain lab equipment, or mental skills, such as spelling

or mathematics computations. Increasing your student's intellectual abilities and development also may be one of your desired outcomes, but you likely will find that there are limits to the degree to which you can address this category directly in your measurable SLOs, as it is difficult to assess, and a commercial test may be needed to obtain a highly valid measurement.

2. **Affective Domain.** This domain is concerned with students' perceptions of the value of the course and the quality of the teaching. These can be assessed with surveys. For example, you may want to develop a survey that measures the student's attitude toward the subject of the course at the beginning of the course compared to attitude at the end of the course. This type of information can be helpful for course evaluation, redesign, and interpretation of test results.

3. **Psychomotor Domain.** This domain is concerned with *perceptual and motor skills*. These skills could include learning a particular dance step, applying instruction for playing a musical instrument, performing a sports maneuver, or creating a sculpture.

Overview of Outcome-Based Assessment

Assessment is the general term for the various procedures that may be used to obtain information for the purpose of improving student learning. A test is one type of assessment instrument. A survey is another type. You may decide to use *tests, surveys, observations, performance measures*, and *group evaluation* as the assessment instruments for your course. Measurement is about assigning numbers to describe how much of some particular ability or characteristic a student has based on the student's responses to items on a particular assessment instrument. In other words, some type of measurement scale is needed in order to determine to what degree students have accomplished the outcomes.

Assessment development is dependent on SLOs that are clearly stated and measurable. *Outcome statements* tell what a student is expected to know and be able to do, and *test items* are written to obtain a measure of the degree to which the student is able to meet the outcome expectations. Thus, the outcomes need to be written so

that they are measurable (i.e., can be measured in some reasonable and effective way). For example, outcome statements that are very broad and global are useful for relating what is expected of students from a high-level view, but test-item development requires outcome statements that are more specific.

When developing an assessment instrument based on *measurable* outcomes it is important to determine the purpose for the instrument. For example, if you want to test art history learning outcomes that require students to *relate common elements* from different periods, then you would miss the mark if the test questions ask the student to simply *identify artists* from different periods. Thus, you would be very limited in being able to use or interpret the test results for the intended purpose, which is to measure the student's ability to *relate common elements* from different periods. In terms of validity, using the test results as a measure of the ability to *identify artists* by period would be a more valid use and interpretation of the test scores than using the test results as a measure of the student's ability to *relate common elements*, as was intended.

One important piece of validity evidence to support the interpretation and use of a test score is obtained by having a good match of the test items to the outcome statements in terms of course content. Another important piece of test-score validity evidence is obtained by matching the test item to the cognitive level that you determine best matches the intent of your learning outcome. For example, if the outcome statement requires a student to *recall important facts*, then you would write items that ask the student to do this. If the outcome statement requires a student to *interpret and make inferences*, then you would write test items that require the student to do these cognitive tasks. If your outcome statement requires a student to *evaluate* or *think critically*, then you would write test items that require the student to do these more complex tasks.

The two main types of test items are *selected-response items*, where the student selects from a list of answer choices, and *constructed-response (CR) items*, where the student writes or constructs the response. The information and guidelines in this book are provided to help you to determine which item type to use, how to construct high-quality SLOs and test items, and how to produce meaningful reports that show student success in terms of attainment of the SLOs.

CHAPTER 1

Developing Student Learning Outcomes

Topic Planning Guide

WHETHER YOU ARE REDESIGNING curriculum and assessment components for an existing course or designing a new course, there are many sources from which you can draw for developing Student Learning Outcomes (SLOs). In addition to your expertise in your discipline, you can draw from the following: existing outcomes (perhaps called objectives or goals in your syllabus), the student and teacher textbook editions, professional accreditation standards, national standards, department and college goals, institutional strategic goals, and other publications by experts in the field.

An integral part of developing SLO statements is to determine the most important (key) topics that need to be covered and map them on a timeline of when they would be addressed during the course. The key topics will provide content structure, and the topics will become part of your broad learning Goals. Because information on all subjects increases each year and textbooks grow larger with each new edition, selecting what is most important is not always an easy task. You don't want to have so many Goals that you have a lot of breadth but insufficient depth, or that the Goals are so numerous that there is no way they could be covered in a semester.

Topic Planning Guide Step One

To facilitate the writing of your first draft of Goal-level outcome statements, make a Topic Planning Guide, as shown in Table 1.1, that identifies the key topics and projects for your course, estimates when during the semester these topics and projects could be

taught, and lists some possible Goal statements. The Goal statements should state in broad terms what you expect students to know and be able to do in relation to the topics and projects. Treat the planning guide as a draft plan to get you started on the SLO development process.

Table 1.1 shows what a first draft of a Topic Planning Guide might look like for a history course. The first column shows the main topics to be covered. The second column contains broad statements of what the writer expects the students to know and do in terms of the main topics listed in the first column. The fourth column contains some statements and terms that help clarify the Goal statements. Remember, step one is just a rough first draft to record some ideas.

Topic Planning Guide Step Two

In step two, shown in Table 1.2, columns one and two are switched so that the emphasis is on the Goal. In this example, the total number of Goals has been reduced to five, which is more manageable, and the *Goal statements* are now clearly the learning expectations. For example, in the second row, Reconstruction, Industrialism, Expansionism, and World War II are now listed under the same Goal of "Demonstrate understanding of facts, chronology, causal factors, and consequences."

Three-Level SLO Model

Now that you have drafted some Goals, topics, and clarifying statements, you are ready to apply the

TABLE 1.1: Topic Planning Guide Step One

Main Topics	Goal Statements	When to Teach	Clarifying Statements
Primary documents	Read primary documents critically and analytically.	Weeks 1–2 and ongoing through semester	Analyze and interpret primary documents Employ primary documents
Reconstruction	Demonstrate understanding of facts and chronology of reconstruction. Understand causal factors and consequences related to reconstruction.	Weeks 2–3	Major events leading up to reconstruction Cause and effect
Industrialism	Know key economic philosophies associated with industrialism.	Week 4	Business terms Explain economic philosophies.
Expansionism	Demonstrate understanding of facts and chronology. Understand causal factors and consequences related to expansionism.	Weeks 5–6	Cause and effect Foreign and domestic policies World War I
The Great Depression	Know the basis for financial depression as exemplified by the Great Depression.	Weeks 7–8	Cause and effect Law of supply and demand Unemployment
World War II	Demonstrate understanding of facts and chronology. Understand causal factors and consequences.	Weeks 9–11	Cause and effect Mobilization New World Holocaust
Historical research and the writing process	Understand the steps and purpose of historical research and the research and the writing process.	Weeks 9–12	Construct written response Apply steps of research process

three-level SLO model (see Box 1.1). Keep in mind that you can always go back and modify your planning guide as needed. As you begin working with the three-level format, you may find that you prefer to do some instructional and courseware planning before you are ready to write your outcomes, or you may find it works best for you to write outcomes prior to or concurrent with the development of your instructional plan and courseware. Regardless of the process you use, in order to have measurable SLOs for which you can write test items, there needs to be some structure to your outcome statements that communicates clearly to students and to any other interested party (e.g., a supervisor, a chair, or an administrator) exactly what students are expected to know and be able to do by the time they have completed your course.

To develop this structure, a three-level SLO Model is recommended. This model allows you to "connect

the dots" from the outcome statements to the test items that measure the outcomes, and then report test results in terms of the outcomes. As you study the examples that follow, keep in mind that the term *Student Learning Outcome* is a general term that includes all three levels of the model, but it does not indicate the particular level or the degree of specificity that is needed in order to write test items in terms of the outcome expectations. The three-level model provides this specificity.

Goal Level

The first and broadest level of the three-level model is the *Goal level*. The outcome statements at this level are directly related to the main topics and goals that you map out for the course. The term *Goal* is used because it is commonly used and understood, but think of the Goal as the

TABLE 1.2: Topic Planning Guide Step Two

Goal Statements	Topics	When to Teach	Clarifying Statements
Read primary documents critically and analytically.	Primary documents	Weeks 1–2 and ongoing through semester	Analyze and interpret primary documents Employ primary documents
Demonstrate understanding of facts, chronology, causal factors, and consequences.	Reconstruction Industrialism Expansionism World War II	Weeks 3–4 Weeks 5–6 Weeks 7–8	Major events Cause and effect policies World War I Mobilization New World Holocaust
Know key economic philosophies.	Industrialism	Week 3	Business terms Explain economic philosophies
Know the basis for financial depression.	The Great Depression	Weeks 8–10	Cause and effect Law of supply and demand Unemployment
Understand the steps and purpose of historical research and the writing process.	Historical research and writing process	Weeks 8–12	Construct written response Apply steps of research process

"overall" or "super" SLO. It is too broad to write items to, but it is the outcome statement that links to department and college goals, which in turn link to institutional Goals. Typically, three to five Goals are sufficient for a course, but there can be more or less than this depending on the type and nature of the course. Student success at the Goal level is typically what you would report to administrators.

General Learning Outcome (GLO) Level

Because the SLO statements at the Goal level are too broad to write items to, each Goal-level statement needs to be broken down into more specific statements that clarify the Goal. Level 2 of the model, called the *General Learning Outcome (GLO) level*, provides the additional clarification. Typically, two to four GLOs are sufficient to clarify a Goal-level statement. The GLO statements are useful for communicating with students about course expectations and typically would appear in your course syllabus. They are also good for reporting overall student success in your course at the department and program levels.

Specific Learning Outcome (sLO) Level

Even though the GLO statements are more specific than the Goal level, they are not specific enough to be made measurable in terms of writing test items. The outcome statements in Level 3 of the model, called the *Specific Learning Outcome* (sLO) level, provide this specificity so that test items can be written directly from them. The small "s" for the specific level is used to avoid confusion with the letters "SLO" which are used to refer generally to *Student Learning Outcomes* at all three levels.

The following is the structure of the three-level model, showing the Goal, GLO, and sLO levels. Remember that all the levels fall under the general term *SLO*.

Web tools that automate procedures recommended in this book are available at outcomesassessment.tools. The Outcome Statement Builder tool allows outcome statements to be written and realigned among levels, automatically realigning the outcome codes and statements. The Outcome Attainment Calculator tool produces specific level and summary outcome attainment reports that can be printed or downloaded as an Excel file.

BOX 1.1: Why the Three-Level Structure?

The three-level structure shown here for writing outcomes is the same structure you will use to write test items and to report test results. In other words, the three-level model allows you to connect the dots from outcome statements to test items to test results.

Each test item used to measure the SLOs is linked to the sLO. For example, let's say that three items on your end-of-course test measure sLO 1.1.1. When you look at your test results, you would know how well your students did on sLO 1.1.1, and you could use this information to make instructional and course redesign decisions.

Since sLOs link to GLOs, you can report student success at the GLO level, and since GLOs link to the Goal level, you can report student success at the Goal level. This process will be explained in more detail in chapter 8.

1. Goal
   1.1. GLO (*General Learning Outcome*)
      1.1.1. sLO (*Specific Learning Outcome*)
      1.1.2. sLO
      1.1.3. sLO
   1.2. GLO
      1.2.1. sLO
      1.2.2. sLO
      1.2.3. sLO

2. Goal
   2.1. GLO
      2.1.1. sLO
      2.1.2. sLO
      2.1.3. sLO
   2.2. GLO
      2.2.1. sLO
      2.2.2. sLO
      2.2.3. sLO
   2.3. GLO
      2.3.1. sLO
      2.3.2. sLO
      2.3.3. sLO

3. Goal
   3.1. GLO
      3.1.1. sLO
      3.1.2. sLO
      3.1.3. sLO
   3.2. GLO
      3.2.1. sLO
      3.2.2. sLO
      3.2.3. sLO

Example of an SLO Structure, Annotated

The SLO example in Box 1.2 shows a course Goal with one of the possible GLOs that clarifies the Goal, plus four sLOs under the GLO that provide the level of specificity needed to write test questions. The annotations in italics are provided for guidance and explanation. A CR item or a select response item could be used to measure the sLO.

The following is a multiple-choice (MC) (selected-response) test item for measuring sLO 1.1.2. The asterisk at the end of option A indicates that A is the correct answer. Almost any MC test question can also be a CR test question requiring a written response.

Question: What is this passage mostly about?

A. Bias and prejudice can affect intellectual growth.*
B. Economic growth is impacted by bias and prejudice.
C. Current thoughts on bias and prejudice lack insight.

Example 1 of the Three-Level SLO Model in Practice

Adapted and modified from a sociology course by Nicole Dash and Brenda McCoy at the University of North Texas, Box 1.3 is an example of the three-level model. It has been shortened from a three-page document that had more than three Goals. Also, there were more GLOs and sLOs for the three Goals than are shown. As was mentioned earlier, between three and five well-worded Goals usually provide adequate domain coverage, but there are always exceptions due to variations in the discipline and course. SLO documents can range in length from two to five pages, depending on the nature of the course

---

BOX 1.2: Example of a Literature Course SLO Structure

1. *Goal*: The student will *understand* literature (from a particular period or genre *by . . .*).

    Note: *The overall Goal typically contains broader category verbs such as* understand, know, *and* apply. *Note the word* by *in the parentheses. Thinking the word* by *is a good strategy to use when thinking about what the GLOs might be under a Goal. Using* by *at the end of the GLO statement is helpful for thinking about what the sLOs might be under the GLO. The idea is that if you can think of anything that would follow the* by, *then those thoughts can become the next level outcome statements. Take out the* by *once the level statements are written so that you can eliminate the "ing" endings on the verbs.*

    1.1. *General Learning Outcome (GLO)*: The student will *demonstrate* accurate, critical, analytic reading of literature [*by* identifying pertinent information, recognizing inferences, and evaluating characters and ideas].

    Note: *sLO statements clarify (break down) the GLO and are specific enough that test questions can easily be written to match them.*

    1.1.1. *Specific learning outcome statement (sLO)*: *Identify* important and supporting details.
    1.1.2. *Specific learning outcome statement (sLO)*: *Determine* the main idea/theme of a passage or piece of literature.
    1.1.3. *Specific learning outcome statement (sLO)*: *Recognize* assumptions and inferences.
    1.1.4. *Specific learning outcome statement (sLO)*: *Explain* how their attitudes and actions define the main characters.

---

content. Mathematics and chemistry, for example, are two of the disciplines that could have many sLOs.

Example 2 of the Three-Level SLO Model in Practice

Box 1.4 is adapted, modified, and shortened from a history course by Elizabeth Turner at the University of North Texas.

Cognitive Categories to Consider When Constructing SLOs

Sources such as Bloom (1956), Linn and Gronlund (2000), and Anderson and Krathwohl (2001) have provided taxonomies, categories, and lists for writing SLOs. I recommend that taxonomies such as Bloom's Taxonomy (Bloom, 1956) be viewed as cognitive tasks that vary in complexity, not that developmentally one category must come before the other. For example, what may be a simple task for someone who has considerable experience with it may be a complex task for someone who is a novice.

The following are brief summaries of some of the most commonly used cognitive categories that are found in sources for writing outcomes. You will probably be referring to this list often when developing your SLOs. I worded the summaries in terms of degree of accomplishment to indicate the measurement perspective and intent of the outcome statement. Item 7, *think critically*, is the most difficult to measure and is covered in greater detail in chapter 7.

The category names are verbs, since verbs are used to write outcome statements. The summaries are not course specific, and each could be a non-course-specific outcome such as are found at the degree program and institutional Goal levels. In other words, at the program level we would want all students who receive a degree from our institution to be able to do these cognitive tasks. At the department and course level, these tasks would be tied to a particular discipline and course content.

1. **Recall knowledge.** The student is required to demonstrate the degree to which he or she can *recall previously learned material, such as facts, terminology, details, and elements.* This may also

---

BOX 1.3: Example 1: Three-Level Structure for a Sociology Course

1. Students will understand the sociological imagination.
    1.1. Describe the features of the sociological perspective.
        1.1.1. Define *sociology*.
        1.1.2. Describe the debunking process.
        1.1.3. Explain the role of the sociologist.
    1.2. Evaluate the societal features that impacted the development of sociological theory.
        1.2.1. Explain the influence of historical events on the development of sociology.
        1.2.2. Summarize the roots of American sociology.
    1.3. Compare (and contrast) the major theoretical approaches in sociology.
        1.3.1. Outline the features of classical theories of sociology.
        1.3.2. Explain contemporary approaches to sociology such as feminist theory.

2. Students will understand social structure and how to study it.
    2.1. Explain the role of culture in society.
        2.1.1. Describe the elements of culture.
        2.1.2. Explain how culture varies.
        2.1.3. Compare how different theoretical approaches view culture.
    2.2. Explain how members of society learn their roles and expectations throughout their life.
        2.2.1. Identify different agents of socialization such as family, media, peers, and schools.
        2.2.2. Delineate the different stages of the life course.
        2.2.3. Give examples of the types of socialization that occur in different life course stages.
    2.3. Demonstrate an understanding of groups in society.
        2.3.1. Name and give examples of types of groups.
        2.3.2. Summarize the influence of social groups.
        2.3.3. Characterize types of organizations in society.
        2.3.4. Compare and contrast different theoretical approaches to groups and organizations.

3. Students will demonstrate critical reasoning regarding the role of social inequality in society.
    3.1. Evaluate how social class impacts life chances and opportunities.
        3.1.1. Compare and contrast different theoretical approaches to class.
        3.1.2. Assess reasons for poverty both in the United States and globally.
        3.1.3. Compare United States class systems with global stratification.
    3.2. Demonstrate an understanding of the social construction of race and ethnicity in the United States and its effects on social dynamics.
        3.2.1. Explain the effect of racial stereotypes.
        3.2.2. Recognize the features of prejudice, discrimination, and racism.
        3.2.3. Compare and contrast different theoretical approaches explaining prejudice and racism.

---

include knowledge of a *process*, such as how to set up a particular chemical experiment.

2. **Comprehend/understand**. The student is required to demonstrate the degree to which the student can *construct meaning from text (or some other source) and can recall, organize, and present it.* This could be constructing meaning

from different genres and understanding *concepts, principles, issues, theories, procedures, organization, arguments,* and so forth.

3. **Apply.** The student is required to demonstrate the degree to which the student *has learned and can apply knowledge such as facts, rules, principles, understanding, concepts, procedures,*

BOX 1.4: Example 2: Three-Level Structure for a History Course

1. Students will demonstrate an understanding of the facts, chronology, and major events of U.S. history from 1865 to 1980.
   1.1. Students will identify significant persons and groups in U.S. history.
      1.1.1. Identify significant persons and groups in U.S. history in connection to major events from 1865 to 1915.
      1.1.2. Identify significant persons and groups in U.S. history in connection to major events from 1915 to 1980.
   1.2. Students will connect factors of causation and consequence to major events in American history.
      1.2.1. Describe the causes and consequences for the implementation of Reconstruction in the South.
      1.2.2. Identify causes and consequences for the development of economic modernization through U.S. industrialization and urbanization from 1865 to 1900.
      1.2.3. Explain the causes and consequences of U.S. imperialism and the nation's rise to world power status.
      1.2.4. Identify the significant problems facing the nation that led to the rise of the progressive era.
      1.2.5. Identify causes for the Great Depression.
      1.2.6. Explain the effectiveness of New Deal programs from 1933 to 1941.
      1.2.7. Describe the changes World War II brought to U.S. domestic and foreign policy.
      1.2.8. Identify the causes and consequences of the Cold War including how U.S. involvement in Korea influenced domestic and international politics.
      1.2.9. Describe the struggle for racial and gender equality and the extension of civil rights to all Americans.
      1.2.10. Describe the Cold War conflicts that resulted in the U.S. military involvement in Vietnam.
2. Students will read critically and analytically.
   2.1 Students will analyze and interpret primary documents.
      2.1.1. Connect and relate the importance of primary documents to historical events.
      2.1.2. Employ primary documents in explaining cause and consequence in the formation of historical events.
3. Students will demonstrate an understanding of the steps and purpose of the historical research and writing process.
   3.1. Students will construct organized coherent written responses to questions regarding major events in American history since 1865.
      3.1.1. Explain causative and/or consequential factors for major events in U.S. history.
      3.1.2 Apply steps of the historical research and writing process.

---

and so forth. This could apply to old or new situations.

4. **Analyze.** The student is required to demonstrate the degree to which the student can *break down the whole into parts in terms of their relevance, purpose, interrelationships, and organizational structure.* This process involves cause-and-effect relationships and also synthesis, to the extent that how the pieces fit back together is part of analyzing their relevance, purpose, and interrelationships.

5. **Synthesize.** The student is required to demonstrate the degree to which the student can *put parts together to form a whole (or a new whole).* This process involves analyzing, classifying, and putting the information together. These learning outcomes require the formulation of new patterns or structures and are considered to be at *a higher cognitive ability* and intellectual level *than comprehension and application.*

6. **Evaluate.** The student is required to demonstrate the degree to which the student can

make *a judgment regarding quality, worth, adequacy, feasibility, or value.* The student likely will have to analyze, interpret, make inferences, determine relevance, distinguish facts, give explanations, and demonstrate sound logical thinking in order to accomplish this objective.

7. **Think critically.** It could be said that CT is involved to some extent in all of the cognitive tasks in the categories listed previously. The measurement interest here is to determine that the student can apply CT as a *process or think critically when evaluating, analyzing, applying, and comprehending.*

The Importance of Verbs

The verb in the outcome statement dictates the action that is expected in order to accomplish the anticipated outcome. Verbs appear at the beginning of outcome statements, often right after introductory phrases, such as *the student will, the student will be able to,* or *at the end of the course the student will be able to.*

The three verbs used most often for Goals and that best capture the intent of the broadest Goal-level requirements are *know, understand,* and *apply.* However, these three words are not exclusively Goal-level verbs. They can also be used at the GLO level, depending on the breadth and depth of what the student is to know, understand, and apply. For example, a student may be expected at the Goal level to *apply strategies to solve certain types of problems,* but to successfully *apply* strategies, the student at the GLO level may also need to be able to *apply* a particular formula, algorithm, or concept. Selecting verbs for outcome levels is always dependent on the relationships between and among the three outcome levels.

The list in Table 1.3 shows verbs that can be used at the GLO or sLO levels, depending on the relationship of the cognitive tasks and expectations at each level. For example, the GLO may require the student to *analyze,* and sLOs under this GLO may require the student to *compare, differentiate,* and *explain.* Then, for another GLO, the student may be required to *explain,* and the sLOs under this GLO may require the student

to *define, illustrate, compare,* and *summarize.* Thus, we see the verb *explain* used in one case for an sLO and in another case for a GLO.

Consider outcome statement development to be the selection of the appropriate action verb plus the use of appropriate and meaningful words in a sentence structure that makes the expectation for the student clear and easy to understand and gets the point across with the fewest number of words (i.e., strive for parsimony). Doing this is not an easy task, particularly when your statement must be (a) *measurable* in terms of constructing test items to test the degree to which the student meets the outcome expectation, (b) *reasonable and fair* in terms of what is taught and how it is taught, and (c) *doable* in terms of what resources and learning experiences are available.

There are many lists of verbs in various formats that can be found in books and on the Web. The list of verbs in Table 1.3 is provided as a quick reference to help you think about what word best fits what you want students to be able to do in terms of your outcome expectations. They can provide initial ideas as you start the outcome writing process. An extended list in the form of question templates is provided in chapter 2.

Guidelines for Writing Measurable Learning Outcomes

When we write outcome statements, we typically think in terms of the end result, as if students are expected to achieve 100% of what is stated, but in reality we know that most students will achieve varying degrees of what is expected. It helps to keep this idea of *degree* in mind when you consider the measurability of your outcome statements—that is, the ability of the statement to allow for the development of reasonable, fair, and doable test items. Also, think of your outcome statements in terms of what you consider to be the most important learning outcomes from the large domain of possible outcomes. Keep in mind that you won't be able to cover everything.

1. Develop a map of what you consider to be the primary focal points of your instruction and course content so that you will have reference points. Indicate approximate timelines

TABLE 1.3: List of Verbs for Writing SLO Statements

Analyze	Debate	Generate	Recognize
Apply	Define	Identify	Recommend
Appraise	Demonstrate	Illustrate	Record
Arrange	Describe	Implement	Relate
Assess	Design	Indicate	Repeat
Associate	Detect	Infer	Report
Build	Determine	Integrate	Restate
Calculate	Develop	Interpret	Review
Check	Diagram	Judge	Revise
Choose	Differentiate	Justify	Schedule
Cite	Discriminate	List	Select
Classify	Discuss	Locate	Separate
Collect	Distinguish	Measure	Sequence
Compare	Draw	Name	Sketch
Complete	Employ	Operate	Solve
Compose	Estimate	Order	Specify
Compute	Evaluate	Organize	Summarize
Construct	Examine	Plan	Tell
Contrast	Exemplify	Predict	Test
Convert	Experiment	Prepare	Transform
Count	Explain	Produce	Translate
Create	Express	Propose	Use
Criticize	Formulate	Quote	Utilize
Critique	Generalize	Rank	Verify
		Rate	Write
		Recall	

as applicable (some outcomes may run across all concepts throughout the year).

2. Use a hierarchical model for the breadth and depth of what you want students to know and be able to do: (a) the overall construct, (b) the big goals, (c) the general outcomes you want to measure, and (d) a breakdown to more specific outcomes to which items will be written.

3. Identify what student behavior you expect to see if a student were to correctly do what

the outcome statement requires. Think about the test format you might use to test the student to determine to what degree the outcome was accomplished. For example, outcomes that require more complex (higher level) thinking on the part of the student may require a CR rather than a selected-response (SR) item and would thus require a rubric (rating scale) to measure the degree of success.

4. As you consider the difficulty of an outcome, remember that the test item you build to measure the outcome can be written so that the item is more difficult or less difficult relative to the difficulty of the task requested in the outcome statement. This range gives you some flexibility in terms of cognitive difficulty when writing the outcome statement.

5. If you want your outcome statement to focus on a specific task, then you need to be careful not to pollute it by mixing in other tasks that are not relevant to that which you want to measure. For example, if you want to specifically measure the degree to which a student can accurately describe the production of a particular chemical solution, then don't include in the outcome statement a requirement that the student defend the use of modern chemistry from a social/political viewpoint. The two outcomes should be measured separately.

6. Use published taxonomies to help with categorizing learning outcomes and selecting verbs for outcome statements, but keep in mind that a taxonomy is not necessarily (or rarely) a developmental hierarchy. Higher level cognition is often involved in achieving a lower level task when the student is at the novice level.

Think about the difficulty of the outcomes as a group. If all of the outcomes are extremely difficult tasks, then the test developed to match the outcomes will likely be extremely difficult (even if you apply item-writing strategies for making items more or less difficult), and you would expect fewer students to succeed (as indicated by test scores). There may be reasons for making all of your outcomes extremely challenging, but typically you should think in terms of what is important, reasonable, and fair when you develop outcomes and assessments, and consider the academic level of the students.

Questions to Ask Yourself When Writing Outcome Statements

1. Does the verb (usually at the beginning) in each outcome statement work to capture what I want the student to know and be able to do?

2. What behavior do I expect the student to exhibit in order to demonstrate to me that the student has achieved the outcome (in terms of the intent of the outcome)?

3. What type of test item will allow the student to show me that the student knows and can do what the outcome states?

Box 1.5 provides additional quality-assurance questions to ask youself when writing outcome statements.

Higher Level Thinking SLOs

Defining Critical Thinking (CT)

The concept of higher order thinking skills became a major educational interest with the publication of Bloom's (1956) *Taxonomy of Educational Objectives.* The top three categories (levels) of the taxonomy, *analysis, synthesis,* and *evaluation,* are typically associated with the terms *higher order thinking skills* and CT. There are different definitions of these terms in the literature, but generally they include skills related to reasoning and logic, which would include tasks or skills related to cognitive tasks such as comparing, classifying, sequencing, cause/effect, drawing conclusions, making predictions, recognizing patterns, analogies, deductive reasoning, inductive reasoning, planning, hypothesizing, and critiquing.

In addition to *critical* thinking, there are other types of thinking found in the literature, such as creative thinking, convergent thinking, divergent thinking, inductive thinking, and deductive thinking. This book takes the position that all of these types of thinking could fall under the term *higher order (level) thinking.* This section will focus on *CT* outcomes.

The following definition of what it takes to be a *critical thinker* contains the elements that can be addressed when measuring CT. Variations of this definition can be found in the literature. As will be argued in chapter 6, the following definition can be addressed with MC as well as written-response test items. The term *ill-structured* in the definition would need to be operationally defined for the student. What is important is that outcome statements based on the definition of CT need to be clearly stated and measurable. A student will be considered proficient in CT when he or she is able

---

BOX 1.5: Quality Assurance Checklist for Outcome Statements

1. ***Does each Goal represent the larger domain of interest?*** For example, if the domain is biology knowledge, then the Goals would have to be related to biology knowledge. If the domain is art history, then the Goals would have to be related to art history.

2. ***Does the Goal statement contain the broader category words compared to the GLO statements?*** For example, for the domain of *biology knowledge*, verbs such as *understand, know,* and *apply* could be used as Goals, but GLO statements would have to be more specific.

3. ***Does the GLO statement further clarify the Goal and make the instructional intent clear?*** For example, the Goal *knows* might be further defined by *identify, define, describe,* and *distinguish between.*

4. ***Does the GLO statement clearly identify in terms of observable and measurable performance the outcome that is expected?*** For example, a GLO statement such as *identify, define, describe, and distinguish among biology terms and concepts related to plant life* clearly tells what type of performance is expected in order to infer that the student *knows.*

5. ***Do the sLOs that clarify a GLO allow test questions to be written that match the sLO?*** For example, to determine that the student can *identify, define, describe, and distinguish among biology terms and concepts related to plant life,* as required by the GLO, the sLO might ask the student to *relate terms to the concepts they represent.*

6. ***Does the sLO statement avoid being so specific that it eliminates flexibility for writing items?*** For example, stating that the student is to *define only terms related to a cell in a specific state of mitosis* would limit the different items that could be written for an sLO that intended to have the student *relate terms to the concepts they represent.*

7. ***Is the sLO statement free of specific scoring criteria so that the outcome statement won't have to be rewritten if the criteria change?*** For example, stating that the student would have to *relate four terms to the concepts they represent and get at least two correct* would mean an outcome rewrite if you decided to go with six terms and three correct.

Note. Adapted from *Measurement and Assessment in Teaching* (8th ed.), by Robert L. Linn and N. E. Gronlund, 2000, Upper Saddle River, NJ: Prentice Hall.

---

to demonstrate the ability to reach a judgment that is judicious and purposive through an engagement process involving analysis, interpretation, evaluation, inference, explanation, and metacognitive self-regulation. The student will demonstrate that he or she can reach sound, objective decisions and resolutions to complex, ill-structured problems by applying reasons and evidence wherever they lead and will do so with a disposition of fairness and open-mindedness (Facione, 2016).

Note that according to the definition, a student needs to be skillful at *analysis, interpretation, evaluation, inference, explanation,* and *meta-cognitive self-regulation,* with the final outcome being a *judgment* as well as *objective decisions* and *resolutions.* These terms give ideas for writing outcome statements.

CT Outcome Statements

The statements in Box 1.6 are SLOs that address higher level thinking, particularly CT. They address what you may want the student to know and be able to do to be certified as a proficient critical thinker. Chapter 2 provides templates for writing test questions, including higher order thinking. The templates can also be used to generate ideas for outcome statements. The following outcomes are in alphabetical order by topic for convenience; the order does not imply an order by importance or cognitive difficulty. The list applies to CR (written) items and to SR (MC) items. Measuring CT with MC items is covered in chapter 7.

BOX 1.6: CT Outcome Statements

Analyze and Organize
Analyze and organize options.
Defend the way options are organized.
Make an analysis of an issue or argument.
Clarify complex ideas.

Argumentation
Describe the flaws (or shortcomings) in an argument or approach to an issue.
Describe flaws and shortcomings in the approach used to make a judgment or conclusion.
Make an argument to support or reject a position.
Identify evidence that supports the validity of an argument.
Explain why a particular argument or position is valid.
Analyze and give reasons for claims used to support an idea or a position.
Analyze and give reasons for evidence provided to support an idea or a position.
Support ideas with relevant reasons and examples.
Make a persuasive argument for or about an issue.
Defend a position taken based on a particular perspective.
Provide relevant reasons and examples to explain and support views.
Provide relevant reasons for why you agree or disagree with a position.

Compare and Contrast
Compare and contrast points of view.
Compare and contrast courses of action.
Compare and contrast strengths of alternative hypotheses.
Compare and contrast the limitations of alternative hypotheses.

Consequences
Determine the likely short-term consequence(s) of a suggestion or recommendation.
Determine the most likely short-term consequence(s) of a suggestion or recommendation.
Determine the likely long-term consequence(s) of a suggestion or recommendation.
Determine the most likely long-term consequence(s) of a suggestion or recommendation.
Determine potential difficulties that are (or may be) associated with a course of action.
Determine the likely short-term consequences of an action or a course of action.
Determine the most likely short-term consequences of an action or a course of action.
Determine the likely long-term consequences of an action or a course of action.
Determine the most likely long-term consequences of an action or a course of action.

Data
Explain data.
Defend data.
Explain data found in tables and figures.
Defend data found in tables and figures.

(Continues)

(Continued)

Fact Versus
Distinguish rational from emotional arguments.
Distinguish fact from opinion.
Distinguish fact from fiction.

Logic Issues
Determine the validity of the logic used in an argument.
Identify flaws and gaps in the logic used in an argument.
Identify flaws and gaps in the logic used to support a position.
Explain the logic used to support a decision or conclusion.
Present reasons why an argument is well reasoned.
State why an argument or position is credible.
Consider the strengths and weaknesses of an argument before making a decision.
Suggest and defend an approach to a problem. Select an option(s) and defend it (them).

Organization of Information
Organize information in a logical way.
Clarify facts and issues that lead to a judgment.
Clarify facts and issues that lead to drawing conclusions.

Pertinent Information
Recognize pertinent questions to ask regarding a conclusion or position taken.
Recognize assumptions and implications.
Recognize assumptions and values that are not clearly stated or implied.
Determine the validity of the logic or underlying meaning of a position or an argument.
Recognize the relationship between what is said and how it is expressed.
Determine the significance of evidence used to make a decision.
Identify possible bias.

Problem, Issue, Conflict
Determine a problem to be investigated.
Identify problems that might arise.
Give reasons why a particular problem is likely to occur.
Give reasons why a particular problem is more likely to occur than others.

Rationale
Provide the rationale for a decision.
Provide the rationale for a decision and include why it is best or better than another decision.
Determine why one rationale is best or better than another.
Explain the basis or rationale for making a particular recommendation.
Identify the contradictory evidence for a suggestion or recommendation.
Present clear and well-thought-out recommendations for a decision.
Present clear and well-thought-out recommendations for a course of action.
Justify a point of view.

(Continues)

(Continued)

Identify specific ideas or sections in a document that support a position.
Identify a questionable assumption.
Identify a critical assumption or issue.
Explain the rationale used to support a decision or conclusion.
Identify the supporting evidence for a conclusion.
Clarify the supporting evidence used for a suggestion or recommendation.
Provide arguments opposing a conclusion. Provide arguments supporting a conclusion.
Explain the rationale used to support a decision or conclusion.

Relevance to Conflict or Problem
Determine which issue(s) is (are) relevant to a conflict or problem.
Determine which information is relevant to a conflict or problem.
Determine which issue(s) is (are) not relevant to a conflict or problem.
Determine which information is not relevant to a conflict or problem.

Resolution and Conflict Resolution
Suggest a course of action to resolve a conflict.
Suggest a course of action to resolve an opposing idea.
Determine which problem, conflict, or issue is the most serious.
Determine why a particular problem, conflict, or issue is the most serious.
Determine potential difficulties or issues associated with a solution to a problem.
Determine different ways of dealing with or solving a problem.

Strategy for Dealing With Information
Explain how best to deal with inadequate information.
Explain how best to deal with conflicting information.
Identify deception used in an argument.
Identify holes or gaps in an argument.
Recognize information that is relevant to an issue.
Recognize information that is not relevant to an issue.
Suggest additional information that would help to resolve an issue.

Value of Suggestions and Recommendations
State why one suggestion or recommendation is better than another (or others).
State why one suggestion or recommendation is likely to be better than another (or others).

CHAPTER 2

Templates for Writing Test Questions

THIS CHAPTER PROVIDES ADDITIONAL help for writing outcome statements and introduces the connection between an outcome and a potential test question. Guidelines for writing test items and test forms are provided in chapters 4 and 5. Reporting test results in terms of outcome statements is covered in chapter 8, which shows the connection between course Goals and institutional Goals. By the end of this book, all the dots will be connected. For now, let's focus on the use of *question templates* for making outcome writing and item writing easier.

The question templates provided at the end this chapter are non-content-specific phrases (or, in some cases, complete questions). The templates are mainly designed to help when you are thinking of possible test questions as you develop test items to measure your outcome statements. The templates also can help when you are having difficulty thinking of possible outcome statements or are thinking of optional ways to state the outcomes.

Since we are talking here about *test questions*, now is an appropriate time to distinguish the parts of a test item. For an SR item, in which the student selects the answer from answer options (choices), there are two major parts: the *question* and the *answer choices (options)*. A CR item that requires a written response, a performance, or a product will typically have *instructions*, a *prompt* (which can be a paragraph or two if needed), and a *question* or a *statement* that gives a command. For a CR, the length and complexity of the parts will depend mostly on the length and complexity of the expected response. The question templates in

this chapter can be used for writing both types of items but are worded more to help with writing multiple-choice items.

Figure 2.1 shows all of the parts of an MC item. Often the test item is called the *test question,* but technically, the *question* is one component of the test *item*. In the diagram, answer choice (option) A is the absolutely and unequivocally correct answer and is therefore the response that is keyed into whatever program is used to score the test items. Answer choices (options) B and C are designed to seem plausible to the test taker as the correct answer, but are in fact not the correct answer, so they are called *foils* or *distractors*. Their purpose is to help make a more valid inference so that the test taker who chooses the correct answer (A) really does know the correct answer. This means the distractors have to be well crafted.

In the example in Figure 2.1, note that the question asks what the passage was "mostly about." In this case, then, answer choices B and C also have to be correct to a degree and thus have to address what the passage is about, but when compared to choice A, only A satisfies the condition of being what the passage is "mostly" about. When all three options are correct to different degrees, the item will typically prove to be of high cognitive difficulty and may be associated with SLOs that are intended to measure higher level thinking (i.e., CT). In other words, the test taker will use more brain cells to get this type of item correct. Chapters 4 and 5 provide guidelines for writing multiple-choice and CR items, respectively. Remember also that almost all MC test questions can be written as CR questions.

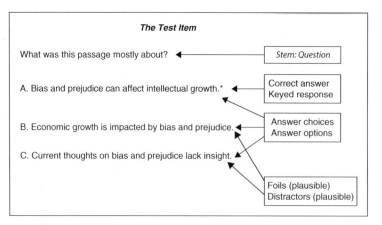

FIGURE 2.1: Anatomy of an MC Item

How to Use the Question Templates

The question templates presented in this chapter are grouped by key words. For example, the templates that are associated with an outcome that requires the student to know the *correct or proper way* to do something are grouped together, and the templates that are associated with *problem/conflict* are grouped together. Two question templates from the list for the *correct or proper way* are:

What (which) is the correct method for____?
What (which) is the proper way to____?

The templates are intended to be used by outcome and item writers to help address the intent of the learning outcome statement. For example, the writer may be writing items that address a Goal that states that the student will *understand the chemical analysis process*. As we know, this Goal is too broad to measure in terms of what students need to know and be able to do, so it needs to be broken down into GLOs, one of which might clarify that to *understand* means that a student knows *proper ways, methods, and procedures for doing a chemical analysis*. This GLO may then be clarified by sLO statements, using the templates such as: *Which is the correct method for . . .?* and *What is the proper way to . . . ?* For these GLOs and sLOs, the test items could require the student to choose the correct answer choice (SR item) or write an answer (CR), depending on the intent of the outcome statement.

For example, the Goal may be to have the student *apply*. If the student can select the *proper way* or *procedure* from the answer options on an MC test, or write down the proper way or procedure for a CR test, then getting the answer correct would allow for an inference that the student can correctly *apply*.

Now, suppose that the intent of the SLO for the *proper way or procedure* requires higher level thinking, and thus requires the item to be more cognitively demanding. For an SR test, the difficulty and cognitive complexity could be increased by requiring the student to select the *best way* for doing something where all the answer choices are correct to some degree, but only one is the absolute <u>*best way*</u>. For a CR test, the student could be offered two or three examples and be asked to tell which provides the <u>*most accurate, correct, or proper procedure, and explain why*</u> or simply be asked to *describe the <u>best</u> way* for doing something.

If the intent of the outcome statement regarding the *proper way* is to require the student to write (construct) the answer to the question so that the student can demonstrate the ability to express in writing and so that the scorer can see how the student thinks in terms of logic and sequence, then the SLO would have to state this, and the test question would have to include these instructions.

The question templates can be used to address the intent of a learning outcome statement in different ways, depending on the creativity of the item writer. So, don't assume that the templates are only for lower level recall-type thinking. Three common cognitive levels to which the templates could apply are *factual/literal, interpretive/inferential,* and *CT/ evaluative.*

Recognize and Identify

You will notice that "recognize" and "identify," which get high usage as sLOs, are not included in the templates. This is because outcome statements using these words would typically require questions that begin with "what" or "which," which you can see are the words that are used for most of the question templates listed but require more than a simple recognition or identification task. A simple use of "what" or "which" would be to determine whether the student knows or can recall "What (or which) is the capital of Texas?" when asked to choose the answer from answer choices or when asked to write the answer. Another example would be to determine whether the student knows "Which diagram shows the molecular structure for ammonia?" when asked to choose the answer from answer choices or when asked to write the answer. Generally, any question used for an MC item can also be used as a CR item, such as a written response.

There is typically some confusion about the interpretation of *recognize* and *identify* when used in an outcome statement. For example, do they mean the same thing, or does one have to come before the other? A simple way to explain this issue is that you have to be able to *recognize* such things as features and characteristics of something or someone in order to be able to *identify* the something or someone. Often the words are used interchangeably. For example, in a police lineup of suspects, the witness is asked to "recognize" or "identify" the suspect, but what is really happening is that the witness first recognizes certain features or characteristics of the suspect so that the witness can then identify the person as the one who committed the crime. Another example, at a more difficult level, would be in a literature class where the student is asked to identify a writer by recognizing the features of the text. In other words, you identify something or someone by what you recognize about them. This difference is something to keep in mind when writing outcome statements that ask the student to recognize and identify.

Describe and Explain

Describe and *explain* are listed as outcomes in the question templates, but it helps to have a clearer understanding of the intent of these outcomes when applying the templates. *Describe* can be related to recognizing and identifying as discussed previously because the intent of a description is to relate characteristics, features, or properties of something. The student could be asked to describe a thing, a concept, a process, a procedure, an event, and so forth, and would then provide facts related to characteristics, features, and properties. To "explain" what is described would require giving reasons for what is described, including answers to "how" and "why" questions.

In other words, you can describe something without giving an explanation, but giving an explanation requires describing. For example, you might ask the student to "describe the steps" in a process, but you would ask the student to "explain how" the process works. Describing the steps would include definitions and a list of the steps. Explaining how would require information about how and why the process works, the intention behind doing the process, and implications and limitations regarding conducting the process. The question templates that follow give examples of questions that could be asked for creating a test item to get at the intent of an outcome statement that uses the words *describe* or *explain.*

Templates for Developing Test Questions

The following question templates are in alphabetical order for convenience, and the order does not indicate cognitive category or difficulty level. All questions have the potential to address various cognitive levels because the test question can be made more or less difficult by how the question is stated and how the answer options are written and manipulated. Certain templates may be used in more than one cognitive category. There is always flexibility in exactly how an item writer decides to apply a particular template. Some of the templates will be more specific to the measurement of literal and factual knowledge, and others are better for addressing a higher level of difficulty, such as interpretive and inferential skills. Others provide what is needed to address CT and other similar higher level cognitive skills.

The cognitive difficulty of any of the question templates can be increased by using qualifiers as shown in Table 2.1. Using qualifiers like "best," "most," or "main" means that all of the answer choices will have a degree of correctness, and you are asking the student to discriminate among the answers to pick the one that is "most" correct. Basically, this is not a different task than when qualifiers are not used—the difference is that without the qualifiers there has to be one absolutely correct answer and the other answer choices are plausible but not correct, and they don't need to have any degree of correctness (i.e., they can be completely wrong). Table 2.1 provides examples of qualifiers so

that you can apply the concept to the question templates.

Question Templates

(Section titles with an asterisk [*] are more adaptable to higher level outcomes.)

TABLE 2.1: Qualifiers for Test Question Difficulty	
Examples of qualifiers to make lower level questions more cognitively demanding	*Examples of qualifiers to make higher level questions more cognitively demanding*
Best description (versus describe)	Best reasoning
Best explanation (versus explain)	Best result
Main reason (versus the reason)	Best recommendation
Main purpose (versus the purpose)	Best decision
Mostly about (versus about)	Best justification
Probably the reason (versus the reason)	Best conclusion
Most like (versus like)	Best argument for
	Best strategy
	Best interpretation of
	Most logical argument
	Most logical result
	Most logical recommendation
	Most representative of
	Most reasonable decision
	Most appropriate
	Best deduction
	Most accurate interpretation

TEMPLATES

Accuracy of interpretation*

Which is the best interpretation of
What (which) is the best interpretation for
Which interpretation of _____ is accurate
Which interpretation of _____ is most accurate based on
Which interpretation of _____ is least accurate based on

Application

What (which) is an application of
What (which) is an application for
What (which) is the application that
How is (are) _____ applied
How is (are) _____ applied to
When is _____ applied
Where is (are)_____applied
Why is (are)_____applied
Why is (are)_____applied when
Why is (are)_____applied to
Which application is appropriate for

Argument*

What (which) (is, was) an argument for
What (which) (is, was) the argument given for
What is (was) the proposal that
What (which) is the main argument
What (which) is the main flaw in the argument that
What (which) is the best argument for
Which offers the best argument for
Which statement could be used as an argument for
Which statement could be used as an argument against
What (which) would be the best argument for
What (which) would be the best argument against
What would be a better argument for
What would be a better argument to support the conclusion that
What (which) is the best argument in support of
What (which) is the best argument in opposition to
What was the strongest argument made
In relation to the rest of the information given, how adequate is the argument that
In relation to the conclusion, why is the argument made inadequate (or weak)
What (which) would be the most reasonable argument for
What (which) would be the most reasonable argument against

Which argument would have the most value for
Which argument would have the most value to
Which argument best justifies the decision to
Which argument best supports the decision to

Argument flaw*

What is a flaw in the argument that
What is a flaw in the argument for
Which statement best describes the flaw in the argument that
Which statement best describes the flaw in the argument for
Which statement best describes the flaw in the position of _____ that

Argument: Hole, flaw, gap in argument or reasoning*

What is a hole in the argument that
What is a hole in the argument for
What is a hole in the argument of
What is a gap in the reasoning that
What is a gap in the reasoning for
What is a gap in the reasoning of
What is a flaw in the argument that
What is a flaw in the argument for
What is a flaw in the argument of

Category, classification, name, definition

What (which) is the correct category of
What (which) is the correct category for
What (which) is the correct classification of
Which is the correct classification for
What (which) would _____ be classified as
What (which) is (are)
Which term means
What (which) is the name of
What (which) is the name for
Which is the correct order for
What (which) is the definition of
What (which) is the definition for

Causation; consequences

What is (are) the result(s) of
What is the significance of
What is (are) the effect(s) of
What causes
What caused
What causes _____ to
What caused _____ to
What is (was) the result of

What would be the result if
What is (are) the consequence(s) of
What is (are) the consequence(s) when
What was (were) the consequence(s) when
What is (are) the reason(s) for
What was (were) the reason(s) for
What is (are) the reason(s) that
What was (were) the reason(s) that
What lead to
What should be done if
What should be done when
Who

Character
What was (person) like
What was (thing) like
What was (character) like
What was the attitude of
Who is (are)
Which conclusion is the most sound
Which conclusion is the most reasonable
In relation to the rest of the information given, how
    adequate is the conclusion that
Which argument best justifies the conclusion that
What would be the most logical decision for
What (which) probably would have been the result if
Which result would be most likely if
Which statement is a non-biased conclusion

Conclusion
What is a logical conclusion from
What (which) is a logical conclusion for
What would be the conclusion if
Which summary statement is the correct conclusion*
What (which) is (was) the logical conclusion drawn
Why is the conclusion drawn logical
Which is the most logical conclusion
Which statement is the fairest conclusion
How would you use
Who did
Why did
What did_____do when
How did

Constraints and barriers*
What constraints were used in the argument that
Which constraint makes the conclusion weak
Which constraints would have to be overcome in
    order to conclude that

Which constraints are most problematic to
What (which) is (are) the barrier(s) to overcoming the
    argument that
Which of the barriers presented most effects
Which of the barriers presented least effects

Correct and proper way
What (which) is the correct way
What (which) is the most effective way
What (which) is the correct way to
What (which) is the correct method for
What (which) is the proper use of
What (which) is the proper way to
What is (are) the way(s) that

Correctness/representativeness
Which statement is correct
Which idea is correct
Which statement/idea should be rejected
What thought aligns with the idea that
Select the statement that represents
Select the statement that best represents
What is consistent with the statement that
Which best restates
Which statement represents the position of
Which statement best represents the position of
Which information is correct

Decisions*
What (which) decision should be made based on
Which decision is the best compromise for
Which decision would be the most reasonable for
Which decision would be the most fair to
Which decision best aligns with the logic that

Describe
What (which) describes
What (which) describes a
What (which) describes the
What (which) is the description for
What (which) is the description of
What (which) best describes
What (which) is the best description for
What (which) describes the way that
Which statement describes
Which statement best describes
Which is the statement that best describes
What (which) describes the position of

Which statement is the best description of
What (which) describes the effect of
Which description fits the
Which description is the best for
Which is an accurate description of
Which description is accurate for

Effects, will happen, did happen
What are the effects of
What are the effects when
What happens when
What happened when
What will happen when
What will happen if
What probably will happen when
What probably will happen if
What probably will happen next
What probably will happen the next time
What probably will _____ do next
What probably will _____ do next time

Event
What was (event) like
Which event was important to
Which event was the most important
What (which) is (was) the event that
Which event indicated that

Example
What (which) is an example of
What (which) is an example that
Which example fits with
Which example shows
Which example best shows

Explains, shows
What (which) explains
Which statement explains
What (which) explains why
Which statement explains what
What (which) explains how
What (which) best explains
What (which) best explains why
What (which) best explains what
What (which) best explains how
What shows that
What best shows that

Fact versus opinion*
Which statement is a fact
Which statement is an opinion
Which statement is fiction

Information needed and missing
What information is needed for
What information is missing
Which information is needed to explain why

Issue or question
What question is raised by
What question would be raised by
Which question was answered when
What (which) issue is (was) raised by
Which issue was closed when
Which issue was closed by

Justifying a point of view*
Which statement best justifies the point of view that
What is the justification for the point of view that
What would be the best justification for the point of
    view that
Which statement best justifies the point of view that
Which statement best justifies the point of view of
Which argument best justifies the position that
Which argument best justifies the conclusion that
Which statement is most representative of
Which statement offers the fairest judgment of
Which statement offers an unbiased judgment of
Which statement offers the most unbiased judgment
    of

Location
What (which) is the location of
What (which) is the correct location of
What (which) is the correct location for
Where is the _____ located
Why is the _____ located
Where must the _____ be located so that
Where did

Logic*
What is a flaw in the logic of
Why is the logic used inadequate in relation to the
    argument that
Why is the logic used inadequate for supporting the
    idea that

What would be the most logical conclusion for the logic that

What would be the most logical result of

Which logic would be most reasonable to use for

Which logic would be most reasonable to support

Which logic would be most effective for

Which logic would be least effective for

Which line of reasoning would have the most value for Meaning

What is the meaning of

What is the meaning for

Which meaning applies

Which meaning is most correct

What is meant by

What did _____ mean by

Modify, change

How could _____ be modified to

How would _____ be modified to

How could (change) be justified

How could _____ be changed so that

What changed when

Option*

Which is the best option

Which is the best option for

Organize, order

What would be the proper arrangement for

What is the proper order for

In what category is (are)

In what category does (do)

Which is the correct category for

Which combination works best

Which design would be used to

Which design would be used for

Parts, elements, features

What is (are) the part(s) of

What is (are) the part(s) for

What are the principal elements of

What (which) are the elements of

What are the products that

What is (are) the feature(s) of

What is (are) the central feature(s)

What does _____ look like

What does (part) do

How does (part) fit with

How does (part) work with the whole

What part is need for

Which part is never needed for

Position*

What (which) is (was) the position of

What (which) is (was) the position taken by

What is (was) the position taken in

What (which) would be an opposing position

What (which) would be an opposing position for

What (which) best describes the position of

What (which) would be a reasonable position to take

What (which) would be the most appropriate position to take

What would be the most appropriate position for

Prediction

What would be changed if

What would happen if

What would _____ do if

What probably would be changed if

What probably would happen if

What probably would _____ do if

What could be a solution to the problem of

What could be a solution to the problem that

Preparation

What (which) is needed to prepare

What is needed to prepare for

How should _____ be prepared

What (which) is the best preparation for

Principle

Which principle applies to

What (which) is the principle of

What (which) is the principle that

What is (are) the principle(s) for

Problem, conflict

What (which) is (was) the main problem

What (which) is (was) the biggest problem

What (which) is (was) the problem when

What (which) is (was) the main problem when

What (which) is the problem that

What (which) was the main conflict
What (which) was the biggest conflict

Procedures, methods, rules
What (which) is (are) the procedure(s) for
What is (are) the appropriate procedure(s) for
What (which) is (are) the proper procedure(s) for
What is (are) the procedure(s) that is (are) used
What (which) is the most appropriate procedure for
What (which) is the appropriate method for
What (which) is the most appropriate method for
What (which) is the process for
What (which) is (are) technique(s) for
What (which) is the best procedure for
What (which) is (are) the rule(s) for
What is the main rule for
What is the most important rule for
What (which) procedure
What (which) method
What (which) rule

Purpose, main idea
What is (was) the purpose of
What is (was) the purpose for
What is (was) the main point
What is (was) the main point of
Which (which) is the idea that
What is (was) the main idea
What is (was) the best idea
What is the best idea for

Rationale*
Which rationale supports the decision that
Which rationale best supports the decision that
Which rationale supports the conclusion that
Which rationale best supports the conclusion that
What rationale was used to support the decision to
What rationale was used to support the conclusion
   that

Rationale, reason
What is the reason that
What (which) is the reason for
What does _____ contribute to
What is essential for

Why did
What explains where
Which statement tells where
Which statement explains where
What explains when
Which statement explains when
What explains how
Which statement explains how
What explains why
Which statement explains why
What shows that
What is the reason for
What is the reason that
What gives a fuller explanation to
Which statement gives a fuller explanation of
Which statement gives a fuller explanation for
Which statement gives the best explanation of
Which statement gives the best explanation for
What (which) is the main reason that

Reaction, Response
What (which) was the reaction of
What (which) was the reaction for
What is (was) the reaction when
What was the reaction by _____ when
Which response shows that
What was the response of
What was the response when

Recommendation*
Which is the best recommendation for achieving the
   goal of
Which is the best recommendation for countering the
   argument that
Which is the best recommendation for countering the
   logic that
Which is the best recommendation for countering the
   conclusion that

Recommendation
What is recommended if
What is recommended when
Why is _____ recommended when
What is the recommendation for
What is the best recommendation for

Relationships

What differentiates _____ from

What distinguishes _____ from

What (which) is the best comparison of

What (which) shows the contrast between

What is _____ like compared to

What is the relationship of _____ to

What (which) shows that

What (which) demonstrates that

What (which) shows how

What (which) demonstrates how

What (which) demonstrates the ability to

What (which) are basic features of

What is the significance of the argument that

CHAPTER 3

Developing an Overall Assessment Plan and Test Blueprint

Developing an Overall Assessment Plan

AFTER YOU COMPLETE A final draft of your SLOs, you are ready to write items that match them. Before you get into the item-writing process, however, it is best to have an Overall Assessment Plan that includes an estimate of how many and what type of items you need and for what purposes, as shown in Table 3.1. Keep in mind that this plan is just a "plan," and you can make changes to it at any time. For example, you may decide after making your instructional plan that you need to make changes to your outcomes and assessments so that your instruction, outcomes, and assessments are better aligned, and thus the plan could change.

In Table 3.1, note that in the *weight* column, the value of the final cumulative exam is worth 50% more, making the *points possible* 90 instead of 60. The mastery quizzes are worth 50% less, making the total *points possible* 60 instead of 120. The final column is provided as a guide for you and your students to consider what may be more or less worthwhile in terms of reward for time invested.

Developing an Outcome-Item Reference Map

It is always good to plan in advance what type of items you might use to measure your outcomes. An Outcome-Item Reference Map (ORM) will help you make decisions about the amount and type of items that may be needed in order to match or align with your SLOs. As shown in Table 3.2, in addition to listing

your outcome statements, all you have to do is put in the number and type of items that you think will be needed to measure each sLO statement, and then indicate what you think the difficulty of the items will be with the letters *L* (low difficulty), *M* (medium difficulty), and *H* (high difficulty). The intent of the outcome statement should drive your estimate of the item difficulty. As a general guide, consider L items to be those that measure more at the literal/factual/recall level. M items would be for measuring more at the interpretive/inferential level, and H items for measuring at the CT/evaluative level.

There is no rule for how many items to have at each of the item difficulty levels for a particular test for a particular course, but typically there will be more L and M items at the undergraduate level, and more M and H items at the upper class and graduate levels. The ORM should be used as a worksheet that can be continuously revised. For initial planning, you will be making your best estimates for the item difficulties, but after you administer a test and look at the percentages of students who got each item correct, then you will be able to change the difficulty designations based on the percentages. When you have actual test results, you may want to consider, for example, 85% to 100% as L items, 70% to 84% as M items, and 70% and below as H items and make adjustments to the ORM as needed. More will be said about item percentages and item analysis in chapter 8.

In the last two columns you can record the number of *short* and/or *long* written responses that you want students to construct. You could also use these columns for performance and product items. Recording

TABLE 3.1: Overall Assessment Plan

Assessment Description		Number of Tests	Total Points	Weight	Points Possible	Impact on Grade
Midterm MC test	50 items	1	50	1	50	High
End-of-course MC exam	50 items	1	50	1	50	High
Final cumulative MC exam	60 items	1	60	1.5	90	Very high
Mastery quizzes at the end of each instructional unit	10 items per person	12	120	.5	60	High
Group discussion at end of course	10 points per person	1	10	1	10	Moderate
Online discussions of various group activities	10 points per discussion	2	20	1	20	Low
Short papers in which students reflect on specific in-class exercises	10 points per paper	3	20	1	30	Moderate
Required survey on student attitude toward the subject of the course	5 points for participation	1	5	1	5	Very low
Total points possible					315	

this information helps when making decisions about whether you need written responses, SR (e.g., MC, or both) items in addition to adequately measuring your SLOs.

When writing your outcomes, there is a requirement that they be "measurable." It is also recommended that you give thought to the difficulty of the task, as is recommended in chapter 1. You need to ask yourself, "What type of behavior do I expect the student to show in order for me to determine the degree to which the student has accomplished this SLO?" In some cases, answering SR items (e.g., MC) would produce sufficient evidence to infer that the student can do the task. In other cases, one or more short or long constructed (written) responses would be needed. Perhaps a performance, such as a presentation or demonstrating the ability to do a physical task, would be needed.

To formalize the relationship among outcome difficulty, item difficulty, and the number of items needed in order to make a valid inference, you can use the information from your ORM to develop a Test Blueprint as shown in Table 3.3. Once the Test Blueprint

is completed, you have a more detailed estimation of whether you have enough items to satisfy your Overall Test Plan, whether you have more items than you need or could possibly administer in a particular period of time or on a particular test, and whether you need more or less of a particular type of item. For example, if there are more outcomes than reasonably can be tested, you will have to decide which are the most important to test. Keep in mind that items are written at the specific outcome level (i.e., sLO), and it would not be unusual to make changes at the GLO level as a result of changes made at the sLO level.

For score reliability purposes, a minimum of four items per GLO is recommended, but this depends on the specificity of the outcome statement. For example, you may determine that for a particularly important or complex outcome you need more than four items or that you need MC items plus a CR item. For another example, you may have two sLOs that are very close in content, so one item each may be sufficient for these sLOs in order to have adequate content coverage at the GLO level.

TABLE 3.2: Outcome-Item Reference Map (ORM)

ORM	*MC Items and Difficulty*			*CR*	
	L	*M*	*H*	*S*	*L*
1. Student(s) will understand the sociological imagination					
1.1 Describe the features of the sociological perspective					
1.1.1 Define *sociology*	1				
1.1.2 Describe the debunking process	2	1			
1.1.3 Explain the role of the sociologist	1	1		1	
1.2 Evaluate the societal features that impacted the development of sociological theory					
1.2.1 Explain the influence of historical events on the development of sociology		1	3		
1.2.2 Summarize the roots of American sociology	1	1	1		
1.3 Compare (and contrast) the major theoretical aproaches in sociology					
1.3.1 Outline the features of classical theories of sociology: functionalism, conflict, and symbolic		2	2		
1.3.2 Define contemporary approaches to sociology such as feminist theory		2			1
2. Student(s) will understand social structure and how to study it					
2.1 Explain the role of culture in society					
2.1.1 Define *culture*	2				
2.1.2 Describe the elements of culture	2				
2.1.3 Explain how culture varies			1	1	
2.1.4 Define *popular culture*	2				
2.1.5 Compare how different theoretical approaches view culture			3		
2.2 Understand how members of society learn their roles and expectations throughout the life course					
2.2.1 Identify different agents of socialization such as family, media, peers, and schools	2				
2.2.2 Delineate the different stages of the life course		2			
2.2.3 Give examples of the types of socialization that occur in different life course stages	2				
2.3 Demonstrate an understanding of groups in society					
2.3.1 Name and give examples of types of groups	2				

(Continues)

TABLE 3.2: *(Continued)*

ORM	MC Items and Difficulty			CR	
	L	M	H	S	L
2.3.2 Summarize the influence of social groups		2	1		
2.3.3 Define types of organizations in society	2				
2.3.4 Compare and contrast different theoretical approaches to groups and organizations		1	1		1
3. Student(s) will demonstrate critical reasoning regarding the role of social inequality in society					
3.1 Evaluate how social class impacts life chances and opportunities					
3.1.1 Determine whether there are opportunities for class mobility in the United States		1	2		
3.1.2 Compare and contrast different theoretical approaches to class		2	2		
3.1.3 Assess reasons for poverty both in the United States and globally		2			
3.1.4 Compare U.S. class systems with global stratification	1	1	1		
3.2 Demonstrate an understanding of the social construction of race and ethnicity in the United States and its effects on social dynamics					
3.2.1 Define *race* and *ethnicity*	2				
3.2.2 Explain the effect of racial stereotypes	1	1	2	1	
3.2.3 Recognize the features of prejudice, discrimination, and racism		2	2		
3.2.4 Compare and contrast different theoretical approaches explaining prejudice and racism					
Total Items	23	22	21	4	2
% MC Items	.35	.33	.32		

Note. Adapted, modified, and shortened from an original form by Nicole Dash and Brenda McCoy, professors at the University of North Texas.

After you complete your Test Blueprint, it is a good idea to change your ORM to align with the blueprint. This way you can use the blueprint as a summary table and use the ORM as a guide for making blueprint decisions. Making improvements and refinements as needed is part of the iterative process when developing quality outcomes and outcome-based assessments.

Developing a Test Blueprint

Now that you have an ORM for the number, type, and difficulty of items that you plan to use for each of your outcome statements, you can decide how many and what types of items you will use to make a particular test form (i.e., the test). Using your ORM as a guide, you now can develop a Test Blueprint for each particular test that you plan to give, based on your Overall Test Plan (Table 3.1). The objective for each test is to have adequate coverage of the outcomes to be tested so that you can make valid inferences about how well the students meet the outcomes. Remember, just as with the development of your SLOs and the development of your Overall Test Plan, if you feel that you need to develop more of your instructional delivery plan and courseware before you develop your Test Blueprint, then do so. You may find that

TABLE 3.3: Test Blueprint with SR and CR Items

	Item Difficulty	*L*	*M*	*H*			
	Cognitive Category	*Literal/ Factual/ Recall*	*Interpretive/ Inferential*	*CT/Evaluative*			
		SR	*SR*	*SR*	*SR Items per GLO*	*SR Items per Goal*	*CR Items per GLO*
Goal 1	GLO 1.1	3	5	2	10	29	2
	GLO 1.2	4	4	2	10		
	GLO 1.3	4	5	0	9		
Goal 2	GLO 2.1	2	3	2	7	15	1
	GLO 2.2	1	5	2	8		
	Items per cognitive category	14	22	8		Total SR items = 44	Total CR items = 3

there are time-saving benefits when you develop your outcomes, test plans, test items, and instructional delivery plans concurrently. The main point is that you need plans and blueprints in order to optimize your tests for their intended use and interpretation so that you can make more valid educational decisions from the test results.

There are many possible scenarios for a Test Blueprint. For example, you may want to develop some formative quizzes and put some of the quiz items on an end-of-course test. For another example, you may want to develop a midsemester test that covers particular outcomes, and an end-of-course test that covers different outcomes, or a comprehensive end-of-course exam that covers the end-of-course outcomes plus some of the midsemester outcomes.

The Test Blueprint is your item development plan. However, once you start writing items, you will probably find that it will be difficult to follow the plan exactly. It is okay to adjust your Test Blueprint as you write items. Your goal is to make sure that you have the best match possible of items to outcomes.

Test developers employ different types of formats for Test Blueprints. The formats in Tables 3.3 through 3.6 are common and useful at the course level, and the

cognitive categories shown are typical, but that doesn't mean you should feel compelled to use these exact categories. You can use cognitive categories from published lists (e.g., lists based on Bloom's categories), or you can invent your own categories. For example, for the cognitive category row in Table 3.3, you might want to use terms like *recalls*, *describes*, *applies*, or *evaluates* (to name a few) rather than what is shown in the example.

Keep in mind as you develop your blueprint that you can make items more or less difficult by the way you word them. For example, a highly difficult Literal/Factual item may prove to be as difficult as a low-difficulty Interpretive/Inferential item. As you are developing the items, you will be making your best estimate of item difficulty in order to match the intent of your SLOs. Keep in mind that you won't have a highly accurate estimate of how difficult an item is or how well it functions until you get the first test administration results back.

Test Blueprint With SR and CR Items
In Table 3.3, two outcome levels are addressed, the Goal level and the GLO level. The first column shows the Goal level, and the second column shows the GLO level. The entries to the right for each GLO show the

TABLE 3.4: Test Blueprint With MC, CR, and One Survey Item

	Item difficulty	Low	Medium	High	Note: In this example all the SR items are MC format, so the "SR" can be replaced with "MC" in the table.				
	Cognitive Category	Literal/ Factual/ Recall	Interpretive/ Inferential	CT/ Evaluative					
		MC	MC	MC	MC Items per GLO	MC Items per Goal	CR Items Short	CR Items Extend	Survey Item
Goal 1	GLO 1.1	3	5	2	10	29			
	GLO 1.2	4	4	2	10				
	GLO 1.3	4	5	0	9		2		
Goal 2	GLO 1.4	2	3	2	7	15	1		
	GLO 1.5	1	5	2	8		1		
	GLO 1.6							1	
	Items per cognitive level	14	22	8		44	4	1	1(20)

TABLE 3.5: Test Blueprint Based on Bloom's Taxonomy

	Know/Recall			Understand	Interpret	Apply	No. of Items	Percent (%) of Items
	Terms	Symbols	Facts	Influence/ Effect	Tables and Charts	Rules/ Formulas		
GLO 1	1	1	1	3	2	3	11	19
GLO 2	1	1	1	5	2	4	14	25
GLO 3	1	2	1	7	1	5	17	30
GLO 4	2	1	1	6	3	2	15	26
Number of Items	5	5	4	21	8	14	57	
Percent (%) of Items	8	8	7	37	15	25		100

number of items that will be used to test the GLO. Each of the items matches a particular sLO. There may be more than one item per sLO, but you can't tell this from the table. For acceptable score reliability, typically at least four items are recommended to measure a GLO, but often more or fewer items will be used if the sLO

	Know/Recall			Understand	Interpret	Apply	No. of Items	Percent (%) of Items
TABLE 3.6: Test Blueprint With GLO Statements								
	Terms	*Symbols*	*Facts*	*Influence/ Effect*	*Tables and Charts*	*Rules/ Formula*		
GLO 1.1 Recognize patterns in atoms that are used to describe matter's physical and chemical properties.	1	1	1	3	2	3	11	26
GLO 1.2 Identify the major types of chemical reactions given reactants and/or products from evidence available.	1	1	1	5	2	4	14	33
GLO 1.3 Discriminate among compounds that form ionic, covalent, metallic, or macromolecular bonds.	1	2	1	7	1	5	17	41
Number of Items	3	4	3	15	5	12	42	
Percent (%) of Items	7	10	7	36	15	25		100

requires it. In the top row are the three levels of difficulty for which items could be classified, and the second row shows the cognitive category (i.e., cognitive tasks that the student would perform) for the item. These categories can vary depending on the discipline and course content, but the three categories shown work well as somewhat universal categories. The letters *SR* stand for *selected response* (e.g., multiple choice), and the *CR* in the last column stands for *constructed response* (e.g., written response). Thus, for Goal 1, GLO 1.1, there are 3 low-difficulty SR items, 5 medium-difficulty SR items, and 2 high-difficulty items, for a total of 10 items for GLO 1.1. Note that in the last column there are 2 CR items for GLO 1.1 and 1 CR item for GLO 2.1.

According to this sample Test Blueprint, there is more emphasis on medium cognitive-level items than on low cognitive-level items (22 compared to 14), and considerably more emphasis on lower-level than higher-level items (14 compared to 8). To put as much emphasis on higher level as lower level, you could easily make an adjustment to your blueprint. Making

minor adjustments after you get into the item-writing process is not a problem, but making major changes can be problematic, so plan well.

Test Blueprint With MC, CR, and One Survey Item
Table 3.4 has the same format and number of MC items as Table 3.3, but notice that there is an addition of two types of CR items, one that requires a short response (perhaps one paragraph), and one that requires an extended response (perhaps two pages or more). Additionally, there is one survey with 20 items associated with the course. This survey could be a survey of the student's attitude toward the course subject or a survey more directly associated with the course SLOs, such as a survey of the need for ethical responsibility if it is a course on ethics. Note also that in the CR extended-item column, one extended CR item is used to measure GLO 1.6. Although the table does not provide identification of this CR item as measuring CT, it may be that GLO 1.6 requires a CT test item if that is the intent of GLO 1.6.

Validity Evidence

The Test Blueprint in Table 3.4 provides specific evidence that your test addresses higher level thinking (CT/evaluative skills), which is typically an institutional-level student learning Goal and thus a program and department Goal. Even if your outcome statements do not specifically state the words *critical thinking* or *critical-thinking skills,* you can demonstrate from the blueprint's *high* column that you do address CT in your course because you have test items that measure it.

Cognitive Taxonomy Blueprint

Table 3.5 shows a blueprint format that is Goal-verb specific, but lacks the specificity of the previously presented blueprints in that no information on the level of item difficulty or the item type is provided. It is Goal-verb specific in that it uses specific Goal verbs such as those found in Bloom's taxonomy, but it is also somewhat restrictive when compared to the three broad cognitive categories used in Tables 3.3 and 3.4. The nouns in the second row of heads in Table 3.5 provide some specificity.

If you are writing a test containing exclusively MC items, say for a chemistry course, and you are using categories such as Bloom's taxonomy (or broad concepts or some other taxonomy), the Table 3.5 format would be useful. Although the format doesn't provide item difficulty levels, you could say, per Bloom's taxonomy, that *know/recall* are the low cognitive difficulty items, *understand* are the medium cognitive difficulty items, and *interpret* and *apply* are the high cognitive difficulty items. Therefore, for GLO 1, you would have three low-difficulty items, three medium-difficulty items, and five high difficulty items. This would be somewhat restrictive, however, in that it implies that as long as you are *interpreting* or *applying* you have a high-difficulty item, which is not always the case. Like in the two previous formats, the numbers in the row of cells are the number of items.

Table 3.6 shows a format in which complete GLO statements are provided. Note that these GLO statements require specific cognitive tasks, such as "Recognize, Identify, and Discriminate," and help make clear what the cells in the rows mean in terms of expected outcomes. If you choose to use this format, keep in mind that it could be a very long document because of the text in the first column, and thus could be cumbersome for use as a summary blueprint.

Steps for Developing MC Test Forms

It is always best practice to do an analysis (see chapter 8) of how the test forms and items functioned after an administration, and then delete any flawed items so that the test results will have a high degree of validity when you use the information for making instructional and grade awarded decisions. The following steps are a good solution when you have not had the time or opportunity to field test and fully validate the items before administering them but need to use them for a summative assessment to assign grades. However, keep in mind that items that haven't been validated or are being used for the first time are really pilot items and likely will need revision after you look at the posttesting item statistics as shown in chapter 7.

1. **Write draft items.** During the draft-item writing stage, give each item its own page (see chapter 4). In this way you can put the whole outcome statement on the page, plus the cognitive level, plus the concept level if applicable, and the complete item with the question and the answer choices. You will then be able to revise the item and add notes as needed. Place an asterisk after the answer choice that is correct for tracking purposes.

2. **Make a test form.** Once the final item revisions are completed, you can cut and paste the items from the one-page format into a test form. Usually, some less difficult items are placed at the beginning of an MC test to motivate the students to continue. Then use some pattern of easy, medium, and hard item difficulty so that students have successes along the way and continue on with the test. The decision to use other patterns, such as the easiest to most difficult item, is up to you, the test developer.

3. **Try out the items.** A relatively quick and easy way to determine how well new items might function is to conduct a developmental tryout. In this process four or five students who have previously taken the course are asked to take the test. They can ask questions during the test. At the end of the testing session, the instructor asks for comments and goes over each of the items so the

group can discuss any issues. Students give input as to why they chose the answer they did and what they think about the items in terms of clarity, format, and content. This tryout session is also a good time to get an initial idea of how long it will take students to finish the test so you can map that into the test instructions, particularly if you decide to make the test a timed test.

4. **Revise items.** Use the results from the developmental tryout to revise your test items. Revisions may include minor to major changes, item deletion, item replacement, and moving the item to another position in the test form. A minor revision might entail simply replacing a word with a more appropriate one. A major revision might be rewriting two of the answer choices or rewriting the question. If you are having trouble revising an item and are spending too much time struggling with it, it may be better to delete the item and start over with a new item.

5. **Field test the items.** Although a minimum of around 200 students is recommended to field test your items and conduct an item analysis (see chapter 8), this may not be feasible for you. An alternative is to have 15–20 students take the test, score the test, and do as much of an item analysis as you can. Make final revisions and save the final version. When using a small sample of students for field testing, expect to do some item revision after the first live administration item analysis results are calculated. Be sure to time the field test to make sure students have a reasonable amount of time to finish the test, or if it is to be a timed test to determine what would be an appropriate time limit.

Following these steps allows you to use items with some degree of confidence even before they have been fully validated. Keep in mind that when using a test form for the first time (without a full item validation), the summative tests that you use to assign grades and make instructional decisions are actually field tests. Any flawed items on these first-time pilot administrations should not be used for assigning grades and making decisions. It is not uncommon for as many as 20% of the items to be flawed on a first administration, and this can be a validity issue regarding the use of the test scores for their intended purposes.

Following the guidelines for writing items that are presented in chapter 4 is very important for developing items that function well, but ultimately you will need to conduct an item analysis to validate your test items, whether the items are SR items or CR items. Chapters 4 through 8 will provide more information on validating test items.

Writing Multiple-Choice Test Items

The Outcome-Based Model

A T THIS POINT, YOU have a model for writing outcome statements at three levels and also a respectable selection of verbs and question templates. So let's say that you have developed your outcome statements, have an overall test plan, and are ready to connect the dots to item writing. You will be pleased to know that the three-level outcome-development model is also the model you use to write items, whether they are SR or CR items. The bottom line for item writing is that the items must match the outcome statement you are measuring, and the item type you chose for measuring the outcome must be the best choice in terms of the outcome statement. Of course, you will also want your instruction to match the outcomes. Figure 4.1 shows these relationships.

It is important to keep in mind that even though it makes sense to start with writing SLOs, followed by item writing, and then developing instructional strategies and courseware, this particular sequence does not always have to be followed. For example, if you are redesigning a course that you have already taught several times, then you typically will already have some objectives or outcomes and test items for the course, and making refinements to align with the three-level model and reworking items following the item-writing guidelines in this chapter may be all you need to do.

At the other end of the spectrum, you have just been assigned a new course, and there is no existing syllabus. In this case, you will probably start with mapping your course topics, Goals, timeline, and

some clarifying statements as was shown in the Topic Planning Guide in chapter 1. Then you will likely be thinking about instructional materials and resources and the pedagogical approach that you want to use as you are drafting your Goals and GLOs.

You will likely find that you will go through an iterative process to get the outcome statements from which you will start to develop your test items. As you get into item development, you may find that you want to test something that you didn't have in your outcome statements. It only makes sense to go back and forth, changing SLOs and items, to get exactly what you want. This process is a continuous improvement model. You will, of course, need to make sure that your instructional model aligns with your SLOs, that you test what you teach, and that you teach what you told the students they would learn as stated in your SLOs.

As you can imagine, there are many other scenarios that may dictate how and when you will connect the dots in Figure 4.1. In this chapter we focus on writing and validating items so that you can make sure you have the best items for measuring your SLOs. Guidelines for writing items are provided. Following the guidelines will help ensure that your items will function well.

To help put things into perspective, the following is the information that would go on a one-page test-item format. It is recommended that you use this one-page format because it contains all the information about a particular test item. The page can be coded, saved, and put into an item bank. Eventually, you will probably have many items in your item bank, and with the proper coding, you can simply pull up the item that you want and paste it into the test form you are

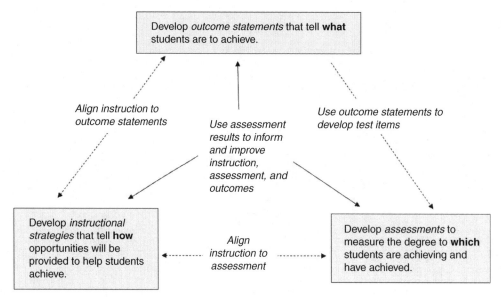

FIGURE 4.1: Diagram of the Outcome-Based Model

developing. The only part you would need to copy and paste into your test form would be the item itself. The rest of the information on the page is for referencing properties of the item.

You may be able to do this process in the particular learning management system (LMS) or other test-development or management program available to you. In these cases you will still want to include as many of the item-to-outcome statement relationships as you can.

Information That Goes on a One-Page Test-Item Writing Form

Box 4.1 is an example of the information that should be included on a one page test-item writing form.

Example of the One-Page Format for Writing Test Items

Box 4.2 is an example (without annotation) of what would be on your one-page form. Note that only one sLO (1.1.1) is selected from all the sLOs that might be listed under GLO 1.1 in your SLO document (or ORM). The other sLOs would be on their own individual one-page sheets (i.e., separate files). LMS programs and other commercial programs

typically have features for creating test items and may allow tagging or labeling for the three outcome levels.

An MC item is used for this example. For a written response, instructions (if any), the prompt, and the item would be provided, which could turn the one-page format into a two-page format or longer. Remember also that the test question shown in the example could also be a CR test item, requiring the student to provide the answer in writing. Components of written-response items are covered in chapter 5.

General Guidelines for Writing MC Test Items

Box 4.3 provides general guidelines for writing MC test items.

Writing MC Test Items

Writing high-quality MC items is not an easy task. In addition to following item-writing guidelines that are considered to be best practices, the item writer must match the item to the SLO statement. If the outcome statement is lacking in terms of measurability, then writing items that address the intent of the outcome statement can become very problematic. This is true whether you are assessing with an MC format or with a scoring rubric for a written response.

BOX 4.1: Instructions for a One-Page Test-Item Writing Form

Course: This is the course ID. For example: *Literature 1010.*

Test name: This is the name of the file in your item bank that contains the items for a specific test form. For example: *End of course cumulative exam.*

Item code: This code includes the Goal, GLO, sLO, and item number and can be used to select the item from the item bank. For example: **G1GLO2S1_M3** would be Goal 1, GLO 2, sLO 1, the difficulty level is "medium," and it is the third item in the bank that matches specific outcome 1.

Goal: This is the broadest outcome statement and contains the broader category words such as *understand, know,* and *apply.* For example: *The student will understand literature (from a particular period or genre).*

GLO: This outcome statement clarifies the Goal statement. For example: *The student will demonstrate accurate, critical, analytic reading of literature.*

sLO: This statement breaks down the GLO statement and is specific enough that items can be easily written to match it. For example, any one of the following could be the sLOs to which MC items could be written: (a) *Determine the main idea/theme of a passage or piece of literature;* (b) *Identify important and supporting details;* and (c) *Recognize inferences, explicit (stated) and implicit (unstated).* Although this chapter is on writing MC items, it should be noted that for a CR (written) item, the following could be the sLOs: (a) *List the sequence of events;* and (b) *Explain in writing the explicit and implicit inferences.*

Cognitive difficulty: Until you have item percentage correct and item analysis data (chapter 8) to give you specific information for making an evidence-based decision, this designation can be whatever you decide is a reasonable estimate of how difficult the item is. For example: A *factual/literal/recall* item would generally be low difficulty. An item that requires *Interpretive/Inferential* skills would be a medium-difficulty item. An item that requires *CT/evaluative* skills would be a high-difficulty item. After you have item-analysis statistics, you can make a more accurate estimate of the item difficulty.

Item: The test *item* is what you copy and paste into your test form. For an SR item (e.g., an MC item), you would create the item question and the answer options. For a constructed (written) response, you would create any instructions, the prompt, and the question, depending on the length of the expected response—a short-answer item would typically require less instruction and a shorter prompt than an extended-response item.

BOX 4.2: Examples of the One-Page Format for Writing Test Items

Course: Literature 1010

Test name: End-of-course cumulative exam.

Item code: G1GLO2S1_M3

Goal 1: The student will *understand* literature (from a particular period or genre).

GLO 1.1: The student will *demonstrate* accurate, critical, analytic reading of literature (by identifying pertinent information, recognizing inferences, and evaluating characters and ideas).

sLO 1.1.1: Determine the main idea/theme of a passage or piece of literature.

Item: What is this passage mostly about?

    A. Bias and prejudice can affect intellectual growth.*
    B. Economic growth is impacted by bias and prejudice.
    C. Current thoughts on bias and prejudice lack insight.

Note. * Indicates the correct answer

BOX 4.3: General Guidelines for Writing MC Test Items

1. What is specified in the learning outcomes will drive the content of the test items. What the SLOs state is what the items should measure.
2. Generally, higher level thinking should be emphasized over recall, but this decision will depend to a great extent on the learning outcome statements.
3. A general rule for writing items is to avoid measuring overly specific and overly general knowledge, but this too will be influenced by the SLO statements.
4. The intent of your SLO statement may require a student to give a written opinion in terms of, for example, a position on an argument, for which you could use the terms *you* and *your* in the instructions and test question. However, keep in mind that when SR test items are used the second person (*you* or *your*) should not be used because it opens the opportunity for personal opinion, which is problematic because then any answer choice could be correct in the student's opinion.
5. Use vocabulary that is appropriate for the group being tested. Keep it consistent with SLO expectations and simple enough that all students will be able to understand it.
6. Edit and proof all items, prompts, and instructions to make sure grammar, punctuation, capitalization, and spelling are correct.
7. Be conservative in your use of words. Don't use excess verbiage. Minimize as much as possible.
8. Make sure the item does not assume racial, class, or gender values or suggest stereotypes.
9. Ensure the item does not contain wording that would offend any group.
10. Make sure minority interests are considered and are well represented.

Source: Adapted from Haladyna (1999)

Many taxonomies and lists of what are termed *concepts*, *goals*, *objectives*, and *outcomes* have been published (e.g., Bloom [1956], Anderson [2001], etc.) and are helpful for writing SLOs. These outcome writing aids are typically in the form of lists, diagrams, and matrices. The idea behind these aids is that what the student is expected to know and be able to do can be related to desired cognitive tasks, difficulty levels, dimensions, and types of knowledge—all of which will help the outcome writer and, ultimately, the item writer.

My recommendation is that writing outcomes, drafting possible items to measure the outcomes, and developing the test plan will work best when done as one integrated process. The reason for this recommendation is that test-item content must match the outcome statement, and the construction of the item that is used to measure the outcome is dependent on the degree of measurability of the outcome statement. For example, a particular outcome may appear to be better measured with a CR item rather than an SR (MC) item. Making a decision whether to change the outcome statement to accommodate an MC format or to measure the outcome with a different format on a different test than the MC test is accomplished more efficiently and effectively when all three components can be manipulated at the same time.

To get an accurate measure of what students know and are able to do in terms of your learning outcome statements, you will want to write items that produce scores that give you the most accurate estimate possible of what you are measuring. Since no particular item will function perfectly, and random things (e.g., a pencil breaks or a computer malfunctions) can occur, there will always be some amount of error in the score. Rules and guidelines have been developed by measurement experts to help minimize the error related to how the test item is written. The following guidelines for writing MC items are common practice in the field. The purpose of these guidelines is to help you develop a test that will produce meaningful and useful scores. As was stated in the acknowledgments, Haladyna (1997, 1999), Osterlind (1998), and Linn and Gronlund (1995, 2000) are the main sources I use for item-development guidelines.

Terminology

As was discussed in chapter 2 and shown in Figure 2.1, the test *item* includes the question or statement (as in a sentence completion format) plus all the *answer choices* and any special instructions or directions that are needed. The *question* or *statement* is also called the *stem* (or, formally, the *stimulus*). The answer *choices* are also called answer *options* (or, formally, the *response alternatives*). The answer choices that are not the correct answer are referred to as *distractors* or *foils*.

Guidelines for Writing the Item Stem

1. *Write the stem as a question.* An incomplete sentence format is seldom a better choice than a question for an item stem. The question-and-answer format works best because it is the normal way we communicate when we ask for information, and it doesn't involve short-term memory issues with having to reconstruct an incomplete sentence for each option (Statman, 1988).

2. *Make the stem as clear as possible so the student knows exactly what is being asked.* Include only the information that is necessary. Don't use excessive verbiage.

3. *Place any directions that you use to accompany text or a graphic above the text or graphic.* Typically, the text or graphic comes before the question. Any directions or instructions included in the item should be unambiguous and offer clear guidance for the student.

4. *Put the main or central idea of what you want to ask in the stem, not in the answer choices.* The choices may be longer than the stem, but the stem should contain all of what you want to ask, and the answer choices should be only the answers (i.e., not words that should be in the questions).

5. *Word the question positively.* Avoid negatives such as *not* or *except*. Using negatives can be confusing to students and can also give an advantage to test-wise students. Using *not* requires students to keep reconstructing in their minds each answer choice, trying to figure out what is not correct as well as what is correct, and this can be confusing. Often, students will read right through the *not* and forget to use the reverse logic needed to answer the question. You may determine that *not* in a particular stem is absolutely needed because otherwise you would have to write too many

additional positive items, but keep the number of negative stems in the test at a minimum. (Osterlind [1998] suggests around 5% at most). If you use a negative, use caps and/or bold font to highlight it.

6. *Make sure that something in the stem doesn't give a clue (cue) that will help the student choose the correct answer.* For example, if you use *child* in the question and *children* for one or two of the incorrect answer choices, you will be giving a clue that the choices with *children* are probably not the correct answer. Clueing can happen within an item and between items. It can be a stem of one item to the stem of another item, an answer choice of one item to an answer choice of another item, or a stem of one item to an answer choice of another item.

7. *Don't make the item opinion based.* That is, don't ask, "In your opinion . . . ?" as this would make any answer choice a possibly correct answer.

8. *Don't write trick questions.* The purpose of a test item is not to trick the student or measure how a student deals with a trick question.

Guidelines for Writing Answer Choices

1. *Traditionally, four (or more) answer choices are used, but in most cases, three options will work better.* Typically, the fourth answer choice (distractor) is the most difficult and time-consuming to write, and, statistically, contributes very little to the information you want from the student's response to the item (Haladyna, 1997, 1999; Rodriguez, 2005).

2. *Make sure that only one of the answer choices is the absolutely correct answer.* Make the other answer choices plausible but incorrect. That is, the student shouldn't be able to easily reject distractors because they obviously lack plausibility. A good strategy is to use typical errors that students make as the distractors.

3. *Ideally, the distractors should be equal in plausibility.* However, it usually becomes increasingly difficult to make each added distractor as plausible as the preceding distractor. Traditionally it has been common practice to use three distractors and one correct answer.

Since in most cases very little additional information is achieved when adding a third distractor, it is usually adequate to stop after two distractors (see #1).

4. *Use a separate page for each item when writing draft answer choices and put the correct answer in the first (A) position, the most plausible incorrect answer (distractor) in the next (B) position, and the next most plausible in the next (C) position.* Ideally, the distractors would be of equal difficulty, but this is difficult to achieve. When you get ready to assemble a test form, you will need to reorder the answer options so that no one position usually has the right answer. A general rule is that no more than two or three of the same letter should appear consecutively. Put an asterisk after the correct answer choice on the one-page item draft for tracking purposes.

5. *Place the answer choices vertically in logical or numerical order.* For example, order a sequence of events from first to last, and order numbers from lowest in value to highest. When making the test form, you may need to reverse this order to be able to vary the position of the correct answers so you don't have more than three (or two if a short test) of any answer choice letter in a row.

6. *Ideally, keep the length of answer choices about equal.* Sometimes this is not possible, but no answer choice should be significantly longer or shorter than the rest of the choices, because the student may be influenced by the length of the answer choice. On the final test form, answer choices should be ordered where possible from shortest to longest or longest to shortest.

7. *Avoid using the choice "none of the above" or "all of the above."* Using these answer choices conflicts with the guideline to have one absolutely correct answer. Although there is not a consensus from research or assessment experts that these choices should be eliminated entirely, it is obvious that identifying two choices as being correct will clue the student to choose *all of the above*. Additionally, the *all of the above* answer choice may have the effect of increasing the difficulty of the item. The student will probably be using a different strategy to address the *all of the above* answer choices than with items that do not offer this choice. You will be on firm ground if you decide to avoid these answer choices. If you decide that *none of the above* or *all of the above* is needed for a particular item, then use caution and think carefully about the other answer choices you create for that item.

8. *Avoid the choice "I don't know."* This can't be considered a plausible distractor because the student isn't given the choice to be distracted and is instead given the option to miss an item that the student may have gotten correct by using partial knowledge or logic. Some experts suggest that this choice may produce a bias in test scores for higher achieving students over lower achieving students (Haladyna, 1997), so it makes sense to eliminate an answer choice that has the potential for producing bias.

9. *Phrase answer choices positively as much as possible.* The use of words such as *not, except, doesn't, didn't, couldn't,* and *wouldn't* will be less problematic in the answer choices compared to their use in the stem, and may work fine (and in some instances make the most sense) if the syntax is well crafted, but the recommended strategy is to consider positive phrasing first.

10. *Avoid giving clues to the right answer in the item options.* This clueing can be within the item and between items. Avoid using terms such as *always, never, none, totally, absolutely,* and *completely* because they set extreme limits and thus can be a clue that they are less likely (or appear to be more likely) to be the correct answer. Similarly, terms such as *often, sometimes, generally, usually,* and *typically* also qualify the answer choice and should be used with caution as they are clues and are more often true.

11. *Using a stem that asks for the "best" answer requires careful wording for the distractors as they all may have a degree of correctness (thus the term* best*) but the correct answer has to be the* best *choice.* It is good to get another expert's opinion on what is the *best* choice and also to try out the item on a few students prior to finalizing the item. Then what you decide

is the correct answer choice will more likely prove to be so (based on an analysis of the item statistics after the item is administered).

12. *Don't make a distractor humorous.* Such a distractor can be a distraction to the real intent of the outcome you are measuring, and has no place in a test for which the results are taken seriously. Students are likely to eliminate the humorous choice and thus reduce the number of choices.

13. *Don't overlap choices.* This applies primarily to ranges in numerical problems. For example, if choice A is 10–20, then B should not be 20–30 but rather should be 21–30.

14. *Keep the content of the answer choices as homogeneous and parallel as possible.* For example, if two of the answer choices are phrases that start with a verb and cover similar content, you would need to make the third choice the same in terms of content and structure. If the third choice is a complete sentence, then it would not be parallel. If the third choice addresses different content, then it would not be homogeneous. However, the answer choices are not limited to the same exact content. For example, three complete-sentence answer choices could have parallel construction, and they could address three different but related pieces of information. One choice could be related to mixtures, one choice could be related to solutions, and one choice could be related to compounds, but all three would be complete sentences with similar syntax. For another example, each of three choices could relate to different art periods, each plausible because of the way each choice is worded and because each is a complete sentence.

Guidelines for Item Format

1. *Choose an item format style and follow it consistently.* That is, be consistent in the way the stem and answer choices are laid out. If you decide to use capital letters at the beginning of lines (even if not a complete sentence) and periods at the end of lines, then be consistent.

2. *Avoid true–false and complex MC formats (where more than one answer choice is correct).*

Haladyna (1999) lists several reasons why the complex MC format is inferior, including the influence of test-taking skills and lower reliability.

3. *List the answer choices vertically rather than horizontally.* This makes them easier to read.

4. *Use three-option MC items.* Statistical probabilities for guessing support this. The probability of getting a three-option item correct by random guessing is .33. However, most guessing is not random but rather applies some form of logical strategy, such as eliminating the least likely answer and making choices between the other two answer choices in terms of a best guess of what makes the most sense. The probability of getting three-option test items correct by only random guessing is very low. For example:

> 2 items correct = .11
> 3 items correct = .04
> 4 items correct = .01
> 5 items correct = .004

The probability of obtaining 70% correct on a well-developed MC test through random guessing alone = .0000356.

"The tradition of using four or five options for multiple-choice items is strong, despite the research evidence suggesting that it is nearly impossible to create selected-response test items with more than about three functional options" (Downing, 2006, p. 292). A study by Haladyna and Downing (1993) shows that three options are typically sufficient, because even in very well-developed tests it is rare that more than three options are statistically functional.

A meta-analysis of 80 years of published empirical studies on the appropriate number of options to use for MC concludes: "MC items should consist of three options, one correct option and two plausible distractors. Using more options does little to improve item and test score statistics and typically results in implausible distractors" (Rodriguez, 2005, p. 11).

If test items are reasonably well constructed and tests have a sufficient number of total items that are appropriately targeted in difficulty to the examinees' ability, test developers can confidently use three-option MC items for most tests of achievement or ability. "Because of their extensive research base, well-written selected-response items can be easily defended against challenges and threats to validity" (Downing, 2006, p. 289).

Box 4.4 provides additional quality-assurance questions to ask youself when writing multiple-choice items.

Two-Column Item-Writing Checklist

Another way to think about the recommended item-writing guidelines that I find helpful is to think in terms of what makes a good item and what must

be avoided. The first column of Table 4.1 is a list of what an item should have and do in order to have high quality and reduce the risk of being flawed. The second column is a list of what must be avoided in order to not have a flawed item. Generally, not following the guidelines in the second column causes more damage than not following the guidelines in the first column. Flawed items result from not following recommended item guidelines and can be identified by item-analysis statistics, which will be discussed in chapter 8.

BOX 4.4: Quality Assurance Checklist for MC Items

1. Item addresses the content and task specified in the outcome statement.
2. Item is written at the stated cognitive level.
3. Question is not unnecessarily wordy.
4. There is only one clearly correct answer.
5. The correct answer is not clued by the question.
6. Negatives are avoided except where absolutely necessary.
7. Question does not contain misleading, ambiguous, or tricky language.
8. Question contains all the information necessary for a response.
9. Options are independent of one another (no clueing).
10. Options do not contain misleading, ambiguous, or tricky language.
11. Options are parallel in structure.
12. Options are of similar length.
13. Options avoid repetitious wording.
14. Distractor options are plausible and reasonable.
15. Options are in logical order.
16. There are no specific determiners, such as *always* and *all* in only one option.
17. There is no option that has the same meaning as another option.
18. There are no all-inclusive options (*all of the above*, *none of the above*).
19. There are no unnecessarily wordy options.
20. Item is free of grammatical errors.

TABLE 4.1: Two-Column Item-Writing Checklist

What makes item high quality	*What must be avoided*
STEM (Question)	**STEM (Question)**
The stem is preferably a question.	Clues in the question that will help the student choose the correct answer choice.
The question is as clear as possible so the student knows exactly what is being asked.	Negatives such as *not* or *except*.
Any directions or instructions included in the item are unambiguous and offer clear guidance.	Opinion-based items.
The main or central idea of what you want to ask is in the stem, not in the answer choices.	Trick questions.
The question (stem) is worded positively.	Options that begin with the same words or phrases (they are put in the stem).
The question (stem) doesn't give a clue or cue that will help the student choose the correct answer.	
OPTIONS (Answer Choices)	**OPTIONS (Answer Choices)**
There are no more than three answer choices.	The phrases *none of the above* or *all of the above*.
Only one of the answer choices is absolutely correct.	The choice *I don't know*.
The distractor answer choices are of equal plausibility.	Negative words such as *not, except, doesn't, didn't,* and *wouldn't*.
The answer choices are placed vertically and in logical or numerical order.	Limiting and qualifying words such as *always, never, none, totally, absolutely,* and *completely*.
The answer choices are phrased positively as much as possible.	Qualifying words such as *often, sometimes, generally, usually,* and *typically*.
There are no clues to the right answer.	Humorous distractors.
The content and structure of the answer choices are as homogeneous and parallel as possible.	Overlapping number ranges in numerical choices.

CHAPTER 5

Writing Constructed-Response Items

Guidelines for Writing Sentence-Completion Items

SENTENCE-COMPLETION ITEMS (CALLED *FILL-IN-THE-BLANK items* by some—but not by measurement experts) typically measure at the recall/factual/literal level.

1. *Make sure that a sentence-completion item type is the most appropriate type to use for the intended learning outcomes.* For example: sentence completion *versus* short answer *versus* multiple choice *versus* extended response.
2. *Provide only one blank.* When it is necessary to use two blanks in the incomplete sentence, then both blanks should be of equal length so that the blank length doesn't give a clue to the student. There may be times when the only way the item will work is to put the blank in the middle of the incomplete sentence, but always try for the end.
3. *Use caution when using exact language in the textbook to construct an item.* Statements from textbooks may become vague or ambiguous when taken out of context and may not address specifically the sLO being measured. There may be times when a textbook statement may work or even be desirable, but choose carefully. For example, a textbook may make a statement that is more of a generalization at the Goal or GLO level, and the context around it supplies the details, in which case you may be able to use the related details as sLOs or test items.

4. *Make sure the item is stated with enough specificity so that only one response is absolutely correct.* For example, if the sLO states that *the student will identify classifications of animals*, then an item that states: *An animal that preys on other animals is a* _____ does not get across that a specific classification is required. To be clearer the statement could be: *An animal that preys on other animals is classified as a* _____.
5. *Make sure the items are free of clues.* Similar to the guidelines for multiple-choice items, make sure there are not inter- or intraitem clues. No clues means that the item is independent and can stand on its own.
6. *Avoid ambiguous, confusing, or vague wording.* This rule applies to all item writing.
7. *Make sure the items are free of spelling and grammatical errors.*

Guidelines for Writing Short-Answer Items

Short-answer-type items also typically measure at the recall/factual/literal level.

1. *Make sure that the item can be answered with a number, symbol, word, or brief phrase.*
2. *Use a direct question.* This guideline applies to short-answer items as well as other item types because this is the form of communication that is most common. An example of a direct question requiring a one-word

short answer is: *What is the first stage of mitosis called?*_____. An example of a direct question that requires a brief phrase for an answer is: *What happens to its mass when water freezes?*

_____

_____.

3. *Structure the item so that a response will be concise.* In other words, like the guideline for multiple-choice items, make sure the central idea is in the question and is complete. The example used previously can be used again to demonstrate this. *What happens to its mass when water freezes?* _____

_____.

4. *If the answer is numerical, make sure the type of answer you want is made clear.* For example: *If a jar of honey weighs 1 pound 6 ounces, how much will four jars weigh?* _____ pounds. _____ ounces. Here, the words *pounds* and *ounces* provide the needed information to make it clear for the test taker.

5. *Make sure the items are free of clues.* Similar to the guideline for multiple-choice items, make sure there are not inter- or intraitem clues. No clues means that the item is independent and can stand on its own.

6. *Avoid ambiguous, confusing, or vague wording.* This rule applies to all item writing.

7. *Make sure the items are free of spelling and grammatical errors.*

Guidelines for Writing Extended-Response Items

Items that require the student to write an extended response to a question is another assessment strategy that can be used to determine the degree to which a student has been successful in meeting the expectations of your SLOs. SR items (e.g., MC) are effective and efficient for measuring factual knowledge and can be crafted to measure at the interpretive/inferential level. Within limitations, well-crafted SR items and particularly item sets can address higher level cognitive skills such as *CT, evaluative skills, argumentation, analysis, application of knowledge,* and *reasoning,* but more often, student writing is used in order to address these skills. Written-response items are also administered to

determine how well the student can express himself or herself in writing. Prompts and questions for extended-response items need to be written so that they are engaging to all students and motivate the production of a response that is extensive enough for scoring.

Student responses to extended-response questions can be one or more pages or can be restricted to one or two paragraphs (called a restricted written response). Since these types of items require a student to construct a written response, a rating scale for scoring is needed. Typically, when there are several categories in a rating scale, the scale is referred to as a rubric.

Most extended-response items contain a *prompt* (also called a *stimulus* or a *passage*) that contains information that is needed in order to respond to the *question.* For example, a prompt might be five lines long and state that there are different ways to evaluate art, depending on the time period in which the artist created the work. Following this prompt, a question would be presented that asks the student to write about the different types of influences that affected art during a particular time period and to compare those influences to influences from another period.

Guidelines for Writing Written-Response Items

1. *Select the SLOs to be measured.* If you are trying to test more outcomes than one prompt can accommodate, then you will need to prioritize the outcomes in terms of importance or possibly make an additional question.

2. *Make sure that the outcome(s) you want to address is (are) reasonable for the length of the response(s) you expect to get.* It is better to have a second prompt than to try to cover too many outcomes with one prompt.

3. *Give enough information in the prompt (stimulus) to make clear the nature of the desired answer.* Make sure the prompt contains all the information the student needs in order to understand the task. Don't assume that the student will be able to read between the lines or figure out what might be missing. Use the prompt to clarify issues that may arise from the way the question is worded.

For example, if the question asks the student to *compare and contrast, summarize, explain,* or *describe,* then give enough information in the prompt to support the question so the student will know what you intend when you use those words.

4. *Avoid questions that are so broad that a knowledgeable student could write several pages on the subject.* For example: *What were the causes of the Vietnam War?*

5. *Make sure the question (or questions if more than one is needed) contains all the information the student needs.* For example, if you expect the student to provide the rationale in addition to taking a position on an argument, then state this in the question. If you expect some type of graphic, then make sure the requirement is clearly stated.

6. *Avoid asking students to tell how they feel about personal things or to relate personal experiences.* The responses will be difficult to score unless the outcome is to demonstrate writing ability rather than to address some specific content.

7. *Use action verbs in the question that encourage extended responses, such as* explain, discuss, illustrate, compare, show, *and* describe. Avoid using verbs like *name, list,* and *identify,* as these words are likely to encourage the student to make lists or give short answers.

8. *It is best to write the scoring rubric at the same time that you write the CR item.* This will allow you to align the item with the rubric anchor points. As you write the prompt and the question, think about what you expect to see in a high-scoring paper and how these expectations are stated in the learning outcomes you are measuring.

Guidelines for Writing Performance-Based Assessments

An extended (or restricted) written response falls into the CR item category. It can be argued that constructing the written response is therefore a performance. Another type of performance is when a student is asked to do tasks like the following:

- Conduct a chemical experiment and explain the results.
- Produce charts and graphs to support an argument.
- Produce a sample of art to demonstrate a particular technique.
- Develop a presentation using a computer program.
- Perform on a musical instrument.

Just as with other item types, performance-based items should be matched to your SLOs. Since performance-based items require a hands-on approach to produce a product or give a performance, instructions and prompts need to be very clear, and a rating scale to score the performance needs to be developed. The guidelines for writing extended-response items and rubrics will apply. Additional guidelines specific to performance-based items are provided here:

1. *Design the performance assessment to match your learning outcomes and what is demonstrated in the classroom.* In other words, make the performance requirements match the SLOs and what is taught.

2. *Select criteria for judging the student's performance that can be reasonably observed, rated, scored, judged, and evaluated.*

3. *Make it clear in the instructions when the student will be evaluated.* Clarify whether the student will be observed and scored periodically, progressively, or when the task is completed.

4. *Make sure that there is a place and setting in which the performance can be presented and that the conditions are the same for all students.*

5. *Determine whether you will observe students individually or in groups.* This may also impact the place and setting for the performance.

6. *Determine how you will rate and score the performance.* For example, you could use checklists, rating scales, journal records, or anecdotal records. You could score the process, the product, and the presentation.

7. *Make sure that important relevant criteria are used for scoring and that there is a match to the SLOs.* Don't include irrelevant or inappropriate criteria.

8. *Clearly communicate in the instructions exactly what the student is expected to do in relation to the learning outcome and how the response is to be structured.* Vague instructions will allow the student to make individual interpretations, which will lead to a wide variety of responses, making it hard to score and unfair to you and/or the student.

9. *Match the performance requirements/criteria to the expected skill level of the student per your SLOs.*

10. *Make sure the assessment can be realistically implemented in relation to cost, space, time, and equipment requirements.* In other words, consider the degree to which the assessment is doable and worth the cost and time.

11. *Make sure your rubrics are well constructed so that you don't leave open to the interpretation of the rater what is the required, expected, or desired performance.*

CHAPTER 6

Writing and Using Scoring Rubrics

YOU WILL NEED TO develop a scoring rubric (scoring guide) to evaluate the quality of your students' CR. Ideally, the rubric should contain a set of ordered categories with descriptions to which student responses can be compared in order to assign a score. In its simplest terms, a rubric is a set of scoring guidelines for evaluating student work. It tells how many points can be awarded for a particular piece of writing or other performance.

Holistic Rubric

A *holistic rubric* has only one general descriptor and provides a single score based on your overall impression of the student's response. For example, a question that asks the student to *compare the art genre for two different periods* can be scored holistically by considering the quantity and quality (including accuracy) of the information provided on a scale of 1 to 4. You would write or have in mind one general description for performance as a whole of what you expect the student to produce. There is typically a high degree of subjectivity in scoring with holistic rubrics. Table 6.1 shows three examples of labels for the degree to which the student can demonstrate mastery of the outcomes that are being tested.

Analytic Rubric

An *analytic rubric* has multiple rating scales, each corresponding to a particular independent learning outcome that added together can provide an overall score. Thus, with an analytic rubric there is a score for each of the outcomes that you expect the student to address, as required by your SLOs. Therefore, you would have a scale for each outcome. For example, if an SLO asks the student to *compare the art genre for two different periods*, with a scoring (rating) scale of 1 to 4 for each of four outcomes, then a total of 16 points is possible. To be analytic, you must provide at least a brief description of what is expected for each outcome. This description will help with assigning the points for student performance on the rating scale for each outcome and will improve the objectivity of the rater doing the scoring. Table 6.2 shows a simple analytic rubric.

In Table 6.2, a student who writes a response that provides the *total number of comparisons* requested, *high-quality* comparisons, the *accurate time periods*, and the correct *artists for the time periods* would obtain 4 points on each outcome for a total of 16 points (the maximum possible). The student who received the scores that are boldface in the table earned 4 points for providing the total number of comparisons requested, 3 points for the quality of the comparisons, 2 points for accuracy of time periods, and 3 points for identifying the correct artist. This student would thus have a total of 12 points (4 + 3 + 2 + 3 = 12). From a diagnostic viewpoint, these scores would indicate that this student is weakest on knowledge of time periods and strongest on knowing enough to be able to make four comparisons.

Analytic Rubric With Proficiency Descriptors

Although providing the outcome for each row, as shown in Table 6.2, helps to score more objectively,

TABLE 6.1: Holistic Scoring Rubric

Score = 1	Score = 2	Score = 3	Score = 4
Beginning	Developing	Accomplished	Exemplary
Unacceptable	Lacking	Adequate	Outstanding
Falls far below	Approaches	Meets	Exceeds

TABLE 6.2: Analytic Rubric Without Descriptors

Outcome	Rating Scale: 1–4				Total
1. Number of comparisons	1	2	3	4	4
2. Quality of comparisons	1	2	**3**	4	3
3. Accuracy of time periods	1	**2**	3	4	2
4. Correct artists of period	1	2	**3**	4	3
				Total	12

to maximize objectivity you need clear descriptors as in the descriptive analytic format shown in Table 6.3. The descriptions at each point on a descriptive analytic scale provide a clear reference point to determine, for example, whether a student's work is *complete to incomplete*, elements are *present to not present*, the logic is *consistent to inconsistent*, the response is *highly clear to unclear*, *highly accurate to inaccurate*, and so forth. Thus, the scoring process becomes more objective because the degree of subjectivity in how the rater might score has been reduced.

It is expected that the outcomes you are scoring on the rubric match your SLOs. The first column in the rubric typically addresses the GLOs. The cells then to some degree address the sLOs that would be under the GLO. The fourth column is the *ideal* of what you expect based on your outcome statements.

Since not all students are likely to achieve the *ideal*, you need to have a clear description for what performance would earn points less than 4. You could choose to set the description for the 3-point column as your *proficient* performance standard, and assign a letter grade of, say, B, for meeting the proficiency

standard you have set. Other letter grades could be assigned relative to the other columns. Using this descriptive type of scoring rubric makes it clear to students what is expected of them and makes it easier to show a student why the student received certain points and overall grade. Ideally, the rubric should be shown to the student prior to the writing assignment so that the student knows what is expected in terms of how you score student performance of your SLOs. Students should have formative assessment experience with the scoring rubric before they are graded on a summative assessment. The prompt and question for a summative assessment would have to be unique, but the outcomes addressed would be the same as the formative assessments.

Typically, a *compensatory scoring method* rather than a conjunctive scoring method is used. With a compensatory scoring method, you average the total points awarded for each general outcome (row). This means that a high score on one of the GLOs can compensate for a low score on another GLO. In other words, you would be assigning letter grades or a pass based on an *average score*. This means that some average scores will have decimals, such as 2.5 or 3.5.

TABLE 6.3: Analytic Scoring Rubric With Proficiency Descriptors

SLO Goal: Write a position paper					
Outcomes	*1*	*2*	*3*	*4*	*Total*
Clarity of position statement	An attempt at a position statement is evident, but it cannot be clearly determined.	Position is not clearly stated and shifts throughout.	Position is clearly stated but the position shifts slightly throughout.	Position is clearly stated and is consistently maintained throughout.	
Structure of the argument	Structure of the argument is weak, and most transitions are weak and unclear.	Structure of the argument is moderately well developed, and many transitions are weak and unclear.	Structure of the argument is moderately well developed, and most transitions are clear.	Structure of the argument is well developed with clear transitions.	
Logic of the argument	Logical argument is weak throughout, and there is very little consistency in supporting statements referring to the original position statement.	A logical argument is maintained to a moderate degree, and supporting statements are weak in referring consistently to the original position statement.	A logical argument is maintained throughout, and supporting statements are moderately consistent in referring to the original position statement.	A logical argument is maintained throughout, and supporting statements are highly consistent in referring to the original position statement.	
Tone of response	Tone contributes little to persuasiveness and is less than 70% consistent throughout.	Tone contributes moderately to persuasiveness and is 70% consistent throughout.	Tone enhances persuasiveness and is 80% consistent throughout.	Tone enhances persuasiveness and is 90% consistent throughout the paper.	
References and supporting evidence	References are missing. Supporting evidence is weak, and in some cases unrelated to position.	References and supporting evidence are less than adequate, and are weak in support of the position.	References and supporting evidence are adequate and moderately support the position.	References and supporting evidence are adequate and strongly support the position.	
				Total points all rows	

With *conjunctive scoring*, you expect a student to obtain the same points on the scale on each of the outcomes in order to get a particular grade or to pass. For example, you might require at least a 3-point response on each of the outcomes in order to pass. To earn an A, you might require a 4-point response on each outcome. You may decide that an average of scores in the 3-point and 4-point columns would qualify as a passing score, in which case you could have average scores with decimals.

With any of these scoring methods, you can weigh the scores for a particular outcome. For example, if you determine that one of the outcomes is worth more points, you could increase the total score for that outcome row by a half point (.5). Likewise, if you determine that one of the outcomes is worth less, then you could decrease the total score for that outcome row by a half point.

Using a descriptive scoring scale to judge the performance for each response per outcome provides diagnostic information that can be used to help individual students and to make instructional and course redesign decisions. For example, if an individual student scores well on all but one outcome, on which the student scores very poorly, then the student can be made aware that improvement is needed for that outcome. If the entire class does very poorly on a particular outcome, then the instructor can determine whether instructional changes or course redesign may be needed.

As was stated previously, an analytic scoring rubric with proficiency descriptors helps to make the scoring process more objective. An analytic rubric is especially helpful for improving agreement consistency when there is more than one rater. Chapter 8 shows how to calculate outcome attainment values from rubric scores.

Setting Rubric Cut Points

Typically, rubric scores are based on the anchor points chosen for the scoring scale. For example, with a four-point scale, the only scores awarded will be a 1, 2, 3, or 4. Because a 3 paper, for example, may be a low, middle, or high 3, or any point in between, it would be more accurate to score the paper on one of the cut-point scales shown in Tables 6.4 and 6.5. In Table 6.4, the proficiency scores awarded are based on a range of points for each point on the four-point scale. In Table 6.5, the proficiency scores awarded are based on points that are midway between the points on the four-point scale. The scoring scale you use to assign grades will depend on your needs and outcome expectations.

Guidelines for Writing Rubrics

Box 6.1 outlines several guidelines for writing rubrics.

TABLE 6.4: Rubric Score Cut Points Set Between Each Point on Scale

1 to 1.9	2 to 2.9	3 to 3.9	4
Far below proficient	Below proficient	Proficient	Exceeds proficiency

TABLE 6.5: Rubric Score Cut Points Set Midway Between Points

1 to 1.4	1.5 to 2.4	2.5 to 3.4	3.5 to 4.0
Far below proficient	Below proficient	Proficient	Exceeds proficiency

BOX 6.1: Guidelines for Writing Rubrics

Determine whether a holistic or analytic scoring is appropriate for your needs. If you want to have subscores for the purpose of increased objectivity, diagnostic intervention, or making changes in instruction at a more fine-grained level, then the analytic scoring will be most appropriate. If you are concerned only with an overall score for a shorter response requirement, then the holistic scoring rubric may work well.

1. Determine how many scoring levels you need to fit your purposes. Table 6.4 and Table 6.5 show four scoring levels, which are usually adequate; however, for particular situations, you may want more or less than four. You can use whatever works best for you as long as you ensure that the levels make sense in terms of being a continuum.

2. Write proficiency descriptors for each level of the rubric, starting with the highest level and working down to the lowest level. It is a good idea to start at the highest level because that is what you expect a successful student will be able to do in response to your learning outcomes. At each succeeding level below the highest level, you will reduce the expectations. For example, if at the highest level a student is expected to address four elements of something and compare them by showing how they are different and how they are the same with a high degree of accuracy, then at the next level down, three elements and a moderate degree of accuracy might be acceptable, and so on through each level.

3. Focus your descriptions on the presence of the quantity and quality that you expect, rather than on the absence of them. For example, if a higher level response requires four elements, and the quality of the response includes a clear description that is highly detailed, then for the next level down, don't state that *one element is missing and the description is less clear*. Rather, state that to meet the level requires *three elements and a description that has a moderate degree of clarity*. However, at the lowest level, it would be appropriate to state that an element is "lacking" or "absent."

4. Keep the elements of the description parallel from performance level to performance level. In other words, if your descriptors include quantity, clarity, and detail, make sure that each of these outcome expectations is included in each performance level descriptor.

5. Avoid the use of words that are vague, such as *interesting, well done, creative, imaginative, sufficient, several, numerous, great, okay*, and other words like these.

6. Be careful not to make the descriptor so detailed and overly specific that it goes beyond the intent of the learning outcome.

CHAPTER 7

Measuring Critical Thinking With Multiple-Choice Items

Rationale, Advantages, and Limitations

THIS CHAPTER FOCUSES ON the MC test format to measure the more cognitively complex tasks associated with higher level thinking, particularly CT. The position of this book is that the ability to think critically engages many higher level cognitive tasks, such as interpreting, making inferences, drawing conclusions, analyzing, and evaluating, and that CT skills are necessary for problem solving.

Rationale

The rationale behind the use of MC items for measuring higher level cognitive tasks such as CT is that they can be a very useful and meaningful surrogate for what is expected from a CR item that is designed to measure similar higher level tasks. A student who obtains a particular score on a written response that is scored with a well-written analytic scoring rubric with descriptors is likely to obtain a comparable score on a well-written set of MC items that address the same learning outcomes.

Advantages

One advantage of using MC items versus rubric-scored CR items is that even with a high-quality scoring rubric that contains clear descriptors for each SLO being scored, it takes a relatively large amount of time to score a written response, particularly an extended response of several paragraphs or pages. In large-enrollment classes, this time consideration is particularly problematic. For example, in a class with 100 students, even scoring at the rate of one student response every 10 minutes would take 16.5 hours of scoring time.

Another advantage of MC items is that the scores they produce are more reliable than written-response test scores. Unavoidably, an amount of subjectivity is tied to a written-response score. MC test scores are objective in that the answer is either correct or not correct and requires no input from a rater for scoring.

Additionally, well-constructed MC items can measure to some degree most of the SLOs that can be measured with the scoring rubric for a written response and typically can cover a broader range of sLOs. Therefore, from a measurement viewpoint, there is a trade-off between an objective score where there is likely to be a degree of limitation to what can be measured, and a subjective score where what can be measured is not as limited but can't include as many sLOs in the scoring rubric.

Furthermore, MC tests are relatively inexpensive to score, and a statistical analysis of how the items functioned following a test administration can be easily obtained. Particularly, they are an efficient way to deal with the assessment needs of large-enrollment classes.

In short, I argue that well-constructed multiple-choice items do a proficient job of assessing subject matter knowledge and varying degrees of higher level thinking. The question templates in chapter 2 provide a feasible way to develop MC items that measure different levels of cognitive difficulty.

Finally, this book takes the position that the scores obtained from a well-constructed set of MC items can be as valid (in terms of use and interpretation) as the scores from a scoring rubric. In other words, it can be argued that an MC from an item set designed to measure CT can provide information for making a valid inference about a student's proficiency at CT comparable to the information provided by a rubric score for a written response.

Limitations

Writing high-quality MC items is not an easy task. It takes skill and creativity to develop items that provide valid scores. Additionally, it is not possible to assess fully with the MC format certain cognitive skills and abilities such as the degree to which a student is consistent in a particular line of reasoning throughout a written response, or the sequential development of a persuasive argument, or the development of an analysis of a particular issue. Making decisions regarding which type of assessment format to use in order to provide the most valid scores for these tasks will depend on how the item writer interprets the intent of the SLOs being measured.

MC items, even when maximized by developing high-quality prompts and item sets, can't address fully the definition of *CT* provided in chapter 1, but capturing the complexity of the definition with a scoring rubric is also challenging and has limitations. The intent and expectations stated in the specific learning outcomes and the intended use and interpretations of the test scores are considerations for making the decision. The issue is not whether an MC format can work, but rather the *degree* to which CT can be measured with an MC format.

What Commercial CT Tests Measure

It is worth noting that the majority of commercial tests that purport to measure CT use MC items. For example, the *Collegiate Assessment of Academic Progress (CAAP)* is a 40-minute test with 32 MC items that measures students' skills in analyzing, evaluating, extending arguments, and drawing conclusions (American College Testing, 2008). The *California Critical Thinking Skills Test (CCTST)* uses scenarios with MC items and expects the test taker to analyze or interpret information to draw accurate and warranted inferences, evaluate inferences and explain why they

represent strong reasoning or weak reasoning and explain why a given evaluation of an inference is strong or weak (Insight Assessment). The *Collegiate Learning Assessment (CLA)* uses open-ended questions designed to measure how well students evaluate and analyze information and draw conclusions on the basis of that analysis, and it claims to assess these skills *holistically*, using rubrics for scoring student performance.

Guidelines for Thinking Critically

The following statements provide reasonable guidelines for thinking critically (Willingham, 2007) and could be used to create SLOs and test items. Here, they have been compiled into a list for ease of use.

In terms of student learning, a student could memorize the statements and try to implement them when engaged in problem-solving in daily life or when being formally tested. I wrote the statements as questions in the second list with the idea that it would be helpful to students (or anyone) to address the guidelines as questions during a problem-solving experience.

> Don't accept the first conclusion that sounds reasonable.
> Look at both sides of an issue.
> Don't discount new evidence that disconfirms my personal ideas.
> Reason from logic rather than passion.
> Support statements with evidence.
> Support claims with evidence.
> Deduce and infer conclusions from available facts.
> Follow evidence to an unbiased conclusion.

> Am I accepting the first conclusion that sounds reasonable?
> Am I failing to look at both sides of an issue?
> Am I discounting new evidence that disconfirms my personal ideas?
> Am I reasoning from passion rather than logic?
> Am I failing to support statements with evidence?
> Am I failing to support claims with evidence?
> Am I failing to deduce and infer conclusions from available facts?
> Am I failing to follow evidence to an unbiased conclusion?

Guidelines for Developing a CT MC Item Set

Typically, it will take a *set* of MC items (item set) to obtain a valid measure of the SLOs. The number of items used will vary depending on two main conditions: the number of sLOs that you intend to measure, and the point at which so much information has been provided in previous items that they provide clues and cues for other items. This limitation can't be avoided and is part of the "trade-off" mentioned earlier. Typically, a set of five to eight items can be reached before the cluing/cueing problem becomes an issue, and this number will vary depending on the length of the prompt, the discipline and content being measured, and the measurement intent of the SLOs. The following guidelines are provided to help maximize the validity of your MC CT items. Examples are provided in the following section.

1. *Keep in mind that the expectation and intent of the outcome statements for CT are that the student can demonstrate the ability to reach sound, objective decisions and resolutions to complex problems by applying CT skills.* The intent of the prompt and the accompanying MC items is that enough information can be obtained to make an inference of the degree to which the student can accomplish the CT tasks.

2. *Identify the SLOs being addressed.* SLOs that address CT can become complex, and whether the Goal is to measure CT *in general* or *within a particular course content* needs to be determined. For example, the learning Goal of *understanding a particular genre of literature* would have learning outcomes that clarify this Goal. If one of the outcomes is to *think critically regarding a particular piece of literature* within the genre, rather than to just *think critically*, then the outcome statements would have to include this content-related intention, and the item set would have to match the outcome statements.

3. *Be clear on the measurement intent.* The intent of the CT SLOs may be to determine (infer) that the student can apply CT as a process, or think critically when evaluating, analyzing, applying, and comprehending. It

is typically assumed that demonstrating this ability in writing is an acceptable way (in terms of the particular SLOs being tested) to support an inference that the student can think critically. When using MC item sets to address CT the Goal is to harvest out of a prospective written-response rubric those elements that can be converted into MC items.

4. *The test items should be a set of items (item set) that addresses the student's thinking in response to the prompt.* Think of the items based on the CT question templates as a representation of or surrogate for what you would expect to obtain from a written response. A written response provides the opportunity to see how a student thinks in terms of the description of a proficient critical thinker given in chapter 1. The same elements that would be scored in the rubric are what you are trying to capture in your item set.

5. *Where appropriate, write student instructions that introduce the student to the task.* These instructions should clarify the outcome expectations for the student. That is, the student should know the intent of the test in terms of the SLOs.

6. *Develop a well-crafted prompt that contains the text and information to which the student is to respond.* A prompt can be as short as five or six sentences to as long as a page or more. It can be one of various genres; for example, *a narrative, a position paper, a persuasive paper, an argument, a scenario, procedures, process, an article, a research article, a historical document,* or *an evaluation.* It should be well structured, engaging, focused on the intended SLOs, and at an appropriate level of difficulty for the intended audience. Here are some examples of content for prompts in different disciplines: To address the outcomes for literature, the prompt might be a critique of a certain literary piece. For a business course, the prompt might be an argument for the use of particular communication skills in specifc business situations. For art, the prompt might be a proposal to acquire an art piece for a specialized type of art museum. For

chemistry, the prompt might be an ill-structured argument for or against using chemicals to control insect damage.

7. *Test score validity is the primary issue that the item writer must address when deciding to use MC items versus a written response.* Therefore, make sure the test items are aligned with the outcomes and definition of *CT* that you are applying. In other words, in comparison to prospective written-response rubric scores, determine to what degree scores obtained from the MC items are valid for making an inference that the student can think critically. A major piece of validity evidence is the degree to which the test items match the intent of the learning outcomes and align with the definition of *CT* that is used. The question templates in chapter 2 are designed to help address this validity issue.

8. *The items (question plus answer options) should meet the best-practices guidelines for writing MC items (see chapter 4).* Pay special attention to the issue of cueing or clueing, in which an item contains cues or clues to the correct answer for another item. Because of clueing issues, you may find that you have to limit your item set to fewer items than you would like (typically at least four to six items can be achieved). The more information presented in items, the more chances there are for clueing.

9. *The questions and answer choices (options) for measuring CT may be much longer than the typical MC questions and answers.* However, avoid excessive verbiage and choose words carefully, but make sure that there is sufficient information in the question and options to address the intent of the outcomes being assessed.

Written-Response Versus MC Items Example

This example demonstrates how MC items can be harvested from a CR item. The Goal in this example is to measure *CT within a particular course content* versus *CT in general*. Although, it could be argued that if you can think critically in terms of course content, then that provides evidence that you can think critically generally.

Prompt

As you can see from the following prompt, enough information is provided so that the student will be able to write a response that is on topic and that will relate to what was taught even though the SLOs are not explicitly stated.

From your readings, you know that one group of Texas congressmen argued in favor of annexation to the United States, arguing that it was the only way to avoid a major conflict with Mexico, which refused to recognize that Texas was no longer a Mexican province. This group suggested that a logical conclusion of recognizing Texas as an independent state would put the United States and Mexico in a state of conflict. The fact is that the United States was not prepared to be in a state of conflict with Mexico at this time. Additionally, the group in favor of annexation argued that diplomatic recognition by the United States would lead to the development of peaceful relations with Mexico and would provide an avenue for developing peaceful relations with the Native American tribes in the area.

From your reading, you also know that another group of congressmen argued against annexation to the United States. They believed that Texas should remain an independent nation. They also believed that Texas should take an aggressive stance against the Native Americans, even to the point of exterminating them. The group felt that as an independent nation, Texas could negotiate on a diplomatic bases and resolve any issues that might arise. They had every intention to do battle with Mexico as needed to keep the Republic of Texas intact. From your reading and class discussions, you also know that the final vote was in favor of annexation. Consider this conclusion and what led up to it when you respond to the test questions.

Test Question

The underlined words in Box 7.1 show the SLOs that were being addressed in terms of CT. Each task that is required of the student in the test question can be found in the question templates in chapter 2. These tasks are also what would be scored in an analytic scoring rubric. Note that the overall SLO here is to prepare a position paper.

> ### BOX 7.1: Test Question With SLOs Underlined
>
> *Based on what you learned and researched about the annexation issue, prepare a paper in which you <u>take a position</u> for or against the annexation proposal. <u>Support</u> your choice with <u>reasoning and logic</u>. <u>Explain</u> why you would vote for or against the proposal to annex. Try to <u>convince</u> the readers of your speech that they should accept your position and vote with you. <u>Analyze</u> the facts before you state your position. Be as objective as you can. Keep your line of <u>thinking logical</u> and <u>draw a conclusion</u> based on the reasoning you present. Give the <u>rationale</u> for your <u>decision</u>. Look for <u>gaps in the logic and reasoning</u> used by the 1845 legislators who supported the position you oppose. <u>Discriminate</u> between <u>fact and opinion</u>. Base your writing on <u>factual evidence</u>, not <u>conjecture</u>. <u>Evaluate</u> the opposing position in terms of <u>fairness and bias</u>.*

Possible MC Test Item Questions

Now, suppose that there are 90 students in the class, and the instructor knows that even with a quality scoring rubric there is not time for her and her one teaching assistant (which would probably take several hours to construct) to do justice to the scoring of the student responses. So, the decision is made that a set of MC items will be used.

To start the item-writing process, the following list of possible MC item test questions (each of which will need answer options) is developed to address CT. The instructor realizes that this approach will not allow the student to "take a position," as required in the CR assignment, but she is willing to sacrifice this aspect of the task because the same CT skills/tasks would be assessed whether the student was for or against the proposal. She also realizes that it will take considerable time to develop the test items, but since they can be used multiple times and the scoring time is reduced almost to zero when using bubble sheets or her institution's LMS program, this becomes a viable option. To maximize the CT intent, she uses qualifier words like *best* and *most*.

1. Which statement *best interprets* the issues faced by the 1845 Texas legislature?

2. Which *argument* has the *best logic* for convincing slave owners to vote for annexation?
3. Which *argument* has the *best logic* for convincing slave owners to vote against annexation?
4. Which *argument* has the *best logic* for convincing non-slave owners to vote for annexation?
5. Which *argument* has the *best logic* for convincing non-slave owners to vote against annexation?
6. Which statement presents the *best argument* for convincing business owners to vote for annexation?
7. Which statement *best describes* the *flaw in the argument* that annexation would lead to peace with the Native Americans?
8. Which statement *best describes* the *flaw in the argument* that annexation would not lead to peace with the Native Americans?
9. Which barriers *most affected* annexation?
10. Which statement *best describes* the *position* of those who wanted to remain a republic?
11. Which *rationale* was used to *support* the position of those who were in favor of annexation?
12. Which *argument best supports* the position of those who wanted to remain a republic?
13. Based on the line of thinking about the value of annexation, which is the *most logical conclusion*?
14. In terms of the business owners' argument for annexation, which statement is the *fact versus opinion*?
15. In terms of the argument that annexation would lead to peace with the Native Americans, which statement is an *opinion versus the facts*?

This list is a good start and may provide enough items for an item set that measures CT. It may need to be split into two sets to avoid clueing and cueing problems. Once the answer options are written, these decisions become easier to make. Remember that CT MC answer options, as well as the question, may be longer than less cognitively demanding MC items.

Short Written Response Converted into MC

In this example it was decided that an MC item would work as well as a short written response to obtain information about the student's knowledge of hospital procedures. In the following text box, only one sLO statement is used.

Converting Item 2 Into a CT Item

By using the word *best* in the question for item number 2 in Box 7.2, making sure that the two plausible options are also true to a degree, and making the keyed response absolutely the *best* answer choice, the items can be converted into an item that requires a degree of critical (higher order) thinking:

Which of the following best explains why surgical instruments in operating rooms are sterilized?

A. To stop bacteria from getting into the body of the patient.*

B. To keep the hospital free from the spread of disease.

C. To comply with the surgical requirements of the hospital.

Vignette With MC Items

Vignettes with MC items are used for medical and legal exams and can be an excellent way to measure higher order thinking in all disciplines. Let's say, for example, that it is important for the students in a landscaping class to demonstrate CT skills, as stated in an SLO, and that the instructor thinks that MC items could get at the intent of the outcome statements as

---

BOX 7.2: CT Test Items Example

Outcomes:

1. Student is able to demonstrate knowledge of hospital procedures.
   1.1. Student will explain the purpose for sterilization in the operating room.
      1.1.1. Student will explain why surgical instruments used in operating rooms are sterilized.

The instructions for scoring the original short-answer written response are that for full credit the student's short answer must include the following information:

1. The need to ensure that there are no bacteria/germs that could infect the patient. For example: *To stop bacteria from getting into the body of a patient and causing infection.*
2. That sterilizing stops the spread of disease. For example: *To keep germs from getting into the body of anyone going in for surgery.*

The following two MC items could be used to obtain the same information.

1. How does sterilizing the surgical instruments used in operating rooms help the patient?

   A. It stops bacteria from getting into the body of the patient.*
   B. It helps the patient recover more quickly.
   C. It provides security to the surgeon performing the operation.

2. Why are surgical instruments that are used in the operating rooms sterilized?

   A. To stop bacteria from getting into an incoming patient.*
   B. To ensure the success of operations performed in the room.
   C. To eliminate the need for postoperative treatment.

Note. * indicates the correct answer

well as a CR item could. The instructor then creates a prompt that is carefully written to include the problem solving and decision-making that the instructor wants to measure. To address higher level thinking, the test items would have to require the student to use CT skills to solve a problem as intended by the outcome statement. Therefore, the instructor decides to write test items that ask the student to determine the *most likely reason* and the *best solution*. The instructor decides that the best way to present the problem is with a vignette (prompt) that provides a real-life situation as shown in Box 7.3.

Typically, a more complex prompt with a *set of* more than the two items would be used to measure CT, but this abbreviated form will provide a simple example.

Discipline-Specific MC Item Set

Now that you have some information on the process for developing MC CT items, let's look at the example of a larger CT item set in Box 7.4. Originally there was a set of eight items that were developed by Tracey Gau, an academic consultant and expert in outcomes and item development in the area of ancient and Renaissance literature. Only four from a set of eight items are used for this example and are printed with her permission.

Note the use of the qualifiers *most, reasonable, fairest,* and *best*. You can also see that the items are measuring CT within a particular course content, which is the usual situation. To measure CT *in general* usually requires the use of a commercial test developed for this

---

BOX 7.3: Example of a Vignette Prompt With CT Items

Outcomes:

   1. Demonstrate the ability to think critically to solve a problem.
      1.1. Apply CT skills to solve a landscaping problem.
         1.1.1. Evaluate the relationship of soil and water absorption.
         1.1.2. Draw appropriate conclusions.

Prompt: A gardener needs to respond to a client's concern that the plants in one of the flower beds tend to look wilted during the summer months, even when the amount of watering time is increased. A large shade tree grows in the middle of the flower bed, and there is mulch on the ground. The client is very reluctant to increase the watering time for the flower bed because it is already much longer than for other beds. Right after watering, the soil appears well watered as deep as five inches, but the next day the bed is dry even deeper than five inches.

Instructions: Answer the following questions based on what you have learned in your landscaping class.

   1. What would you tell the gardener is the *most likely reason* for the dryness of the water bed?

      A. The water is seeping past the flowers' roots more quickly than the flower plants can capture it.
      B. The roots of the tree are sucking up the water and drying the soil, thus depriving the plants.*
      C. The summer heat is drying out the soil too quickly for plant roots to capture the water.

   2. What would you tell the gardener is the *best solution* to the watering issue?

      A. Increase the watering time to whatever it takes to keep the soil moist.
      B. Change out the sprinkler heads to provide more water in the same amount of time.*
      C. Add a thicker layer of mulch to the flower bed to keep in the moisture.

Note. * indicates the correct answer

purpose. However, CT within a course content will provide evidence that CT is assessed when addressing department Goals, institutional strategic Goals, and accreditation organizations that require CT as an SLO.

Measuring General CT

To obtain a measure of a student's CT ability not specifically related to course content, it may be best to use a commercially developed instrument in which

---

BOX 7.4: Example of Using a Set of Measure CT

Outcomes:

1. Undergraduate students in English will be able to read critically and analytically.
    1.1. Analyze, evaluate, interpret, and synthesize representative texts from the Eastern and Western traditions and relate them to their literary and cultural contexts.
        1.1.1. Compare and contrast major literary themes and figures and their situations and decisions.

Prompt. In reading representative ancient epics of the Western and Eastern traditions, we see that while some characteristic aspects, actions, and attitudes overlap, each culture also privileges different virtues, motivations, and worldviews. For example, using the *Iliad* and the *Ramayana*, we can contrast the Greek depiction of *fate* with the Indian depiction of *daiva* as well as contrast the Greek *heroic code* with the Indian code of *dharma* as seen in Rama's actions. Consider this information when answering the following questions.

1. What leadership characteristic praised in the Indian epic the *Ramayana* is *most often* characterized as a fault or weakness in Greek epics like the *Iliad*?

    A. Compassion*
    B. Courage
    C. Wisdom

2. According to *dharma*, what would be a *reasonable action* for Rama to take when faced with an unfair request by a parent or god?

    A. Argue his case calmly and rationally
    B. Obey without hesitation*
    C. Resist the injustice by preparing for battle

3. The Greek understanding of fate differs from the Indian concept of daiva. Which statement is the *fairest* description of the difference?

    A. Humans determine their own fate, whereas daiva is the guiding principle of human conduct.
    B. The gods control fate, but daiva is determined by one's own actions.
    C. Fate is understood as capricious, whereas daiva is purposeful.*

4. Which is *the best argument* in support of Achilles' withdrawal from the battle as depicted in the *Iliad*?

    A. Agamemnon violates the code of *aidos* in taking Achilles' war prize, Briseis.*
    B. Achilles' *kudos* is an understandable reaction to Agamemnon's action.
    C. Agamemnon's *hate* leads him to abuse his power.

Note. * indicates the correct answer

---

the items and test scores have been validated for their intended use. This type of validation requires sophisticated psychometrics. Tests of this caliber can be found with a Google search.

As was previously stated, commercial critical-thinking tests employ MC and CR test formats. One approach is to have the student read one or more passages or documents, which are the prompt. The student is asked to read the prompt and respond in writing or answer MC items. For example, the student could be presented with three positions on the use of nuclear power versus solar energy. The SLOs would require the student to demonstrate higher level cognitive skills, such as analyzing, comparing and contrasting, synthesizing, thinking logically, and drawing conclusions.

To give you a flavor of how non-course-content measurement of CT might work in terms of the definition of *CT* and the question templates in chapter 2, the following MC example is provided. Note that the one-page prompt presented includes different viewpoints on a traffic incident. There is no claim being made here that the example could replace a commercial test in which test items and the test scores produced have been validated for their intended use, because this CT test is my invention for purposes of illustration, and a full validation study has not been conducted. An instructor-developed test to measure student CT using a small set of validated items (see chapter 8) would, however, provide validity evidence that the SLOs that require a student to think critically are being addressed and that the test items match the expectations of the sLOs that require CT skills.

In the example that follows, *instructions* are provided, followed by a *prompt* that has four parts: facts, one driver's view, another driver's view, and the view of the police. The question templates in chapter 2 that have an asterisk to designate them as higher level thinking questions were used to write the items.

Outcomes measured:

1. Identify a critical assumption or issue.
2. Identify flaws and gaps in the logic used in an argument.
3. Determine what arguments are needed to support or reject a position.
4. Distinguish fact from opinion.
5. Explain the logic used to support a decision or conclusion.
6. Determine which information is relevant to a conflict or problem.
7. Determine the validity of the logic used in an argument.

Instructions

Read the following information about a traffic incident on a university campus, and then answer the questions in Box 7.5. The purpose of this test is to measure your ability to think critically about and evaluate circumstances, claims, and opinions regarding a driving accident and to come to a logical conclusion regarding the final outcome.

Facts

While driving on campus, Logan did not come to a full stop at a stop sign before turning right. He didn't notice that a pedestrian was about to step into the crosswalk. To avoid the possibility of hitting the pedestrian, he swerved out of the way and forced Star, who was driving in the opposite direction, to drive over the curb and onto the sidewalk, forcing a walker on the sidewalk to fall. The walker sustained only a minor bruise and a couple of scratches from falling into some bushes but was too shocked to stand up and walk. There was no damage to either car. Logan, Star, and the walker were students at the university. Star wrote down Logan's license number. The speed limit on the campus is 20 mph.

Star's Position

Star immediately got out of her car and told Logan how stupid he was and that driving rules were created for a purpose. Star then calmed down a little and explained to Logan that if he had simply made a complete stop, then he would have seen the pedestrian trying to cross the street, which the pedestrian had every right to do because the crosswalk was clearly marked, and the accident could have been avoided.

Logan's Position

Logan rejected Star's conclusion on the basis that there was no way to know that the pedestrian would not have stepped off the curb anyway. Logan said that if Star hadn't been speeding, then he could have safely swerved around the pedestrian and avoided any injury. Logan insisted that it was his right to take evasive action as he deemed necessary and that Star had usurped that right; therefore, the fault lay squarely on Star. Logan then suggested that Star should take the injured person to the university clinic and that it was not necessary to call the police because everything could be taken care of by the university since they were all registered students. Additionally, Logan explained that there was no need to call the police because there was no actual damage to the cars. Logan said that since he was not the one who hit the walker he did not have to stay around, so he drove off.

Police Position

Star took the injured walker to the university infirmary and called the police. She explained what happened in detail to the responding officer and told how Logan was the cause of the accident. The officer interviewed the injured walker, talked with Logan by phone, and concluded that Logan's rationale for his actions was defensible and that both drivers were equally responsible. Star received a ticket for reckless driving, and Logan received a warning.

Star also received a phone call from Logan's attorney that Logan was considering a lawsuit for defamation of character for falsely accusing Logan of being the cause of the accident.

Based on the information provided, answer the questions listed in Box 7.5.

Converting a Rubric into a Three-Level Model

One of the AAC&U LEAP VALUE rubrics that is often used as a course requirement is the Critical Thinking Rubric. Box 7.6 shows the content of the CT rubric converted to a three-level structure so that MC items can be developed for the sLO-level statements. The content is as close to the words and phrases in the VALUE rubric as possible. The conversion is also a demonstration of how the three-level structure can be used to zero in on particular sections of the outcomes to be taught and tested. The structure would be useful as a guide even if a written response was required, because the GLO statements could be used for the rubric rows (of course, the sLOs would still be taught).

BOX 7.5: CT Item Set for the Traffic Accident Prompt

1. Which *best* describes the position taken by Star?

    A. If Logan had obeyed driving rules, then the accident would have been avoided.*
    B. If Logan had come to a full stop, then the accident could have been avoided.
    C. If Logan had provided the pedestrian his legal rights, then there would be no issue.

2. What *best* describes a flaw in Logan's argument that he had the right to take evasive action?

    A. His premise for taking the action was not based on facts.*
    B. What a person is thinking of doing is not reliable.
    C. A cause-and-effect relation for evasive action cannot be established.

3. Which would be the *best argument* to refute the decision of the police officer that Star should receive a ticket?

    A. Logan was not formally interviewed, so the officer's decision is biased due to lack of evidence.*
    B. The officer was not at the scene of the accident so he has insufficient evidence from which to draw conclusions.
    C. There is no evidence that Star was speeding and therefore contributed to the cause of the accident.

4. Which statement is an opinion?

    A. Star was speeding when she ran the walker into the bushes.*
    B. It was appropriate for Star to take the pedestrian to the infirmary.
    C. Logan should have come to a complete stop at the stop sign.

5. What *best* states the strategy that was used by Logan to devalue the logic that Star offered?

    A. He moved the focus of the issue from the rights of the pedestrian to the rights of Logan as a driver.*
    B. He referenced speeding on campus and capitalized on this to show Star as an offender.
    C. He played off the injury to the walker to make Star feel responsible for the accident.

6. What information would be *most relevant* to a defense by Star if Logan decided to sue her for defamation of character?

    A. The police officer concluded that both drivers were equally responsible.*
    B. Logan said that he didn't need to stay and left the scene of an accident.
    C. Star was the one who called the police to report the accident.

7. Which conclusion regarding the disposition of the case by the police officer is *most sound* (i.e., unbiased, logical, and fair)?

    A. It was unfair for the police officer to give Star a ticket for reckless driving.*
    B. Logan should have received a ticket for reckless driving rather than Star.
    C. Neither Star nor Logan should have received a ticket or a warning.

Note. * indicates the correct answer

BOX 7.6: Three-Level Outcome Statements for the AA&U LEAP Critical Thinking VALUE Rubric

1. Student will demonstrate the ability to think critically by completing a comprehensive exploration of issues, ideas, artifacts, and events before accepting or formulating an opinion or a conclusion.
   1.1. Student will explain the issues.
      1.1.1. State the problem or issue clearly.
      1.1.2. Give a comprehensive description of the problem or issue.
      1.1.3. Provide all relevant information necessary for full understanding.
   1.2. Student will provide evidence that supports a point of view or conclusion.
      1.2.1. Select and interpret/evaluate source information.
      1.2.2. Develop a comprehensive analysis or synthesis.
      1.2.3. Question thoroughly the viewpoint of experts.
   1.3. Student will address the influence of context and assumptions.
      1.3.1. Systematically and methodically analyze assumptions of self and others.
      1.3.2. Evaluate the relevance of contexts when presenting a position.
   1.4. Student will provide a specific position (perspective, thesis/hypothesis).
      1.4.1. State a position in a way that is imaginative.
      1.4.2. State a position that takes into account the complexities of an issue.
      1.4.3. Acknowledge the limits of the position taken.
      1.4.4. Synthesize within the position the point of view of others.
   1.5. Student will state a conclusion(s) and related outcome(s) (implications and consequences).
      1.5.1. State conclusion(s) and outcome(s) that are logical.
      1.5.2. State conclusion(s) and outcome(s) that reflect informed evaluation.
      1.5.3. State conclusion(s) and outcome(s) that reflect ability to prioritize evidence and perspectives.

CHAPTER 8

Reporting Results With the Three-Level Model

RESULTS FROM ASSESSMENTS ARE typically used to assign grades to students based on their test scores and to see how the class as a whole did based on an average of the test scores. At the individual level, the primary interest is on the number of items for which the student chose the correct answer or achieved a particular point on a scoring rubric scale. For individuals, the inference is that the higher the score, the higher the student's attainment of the outcomes. For the class the inference is the same. However, the student's score does not indicate which outcomes the student achieved or attained and to what degree. For example, a student may have attained a high degree on 75% of the outcomes and failed completely on 25% of the outcomes and still got a percentage correct score that would award the student a passing grade. This same logic applies to the class as a whole.

For diagnostic purposes, it would be ideal if the assessment results could show how well each student attained each sLO. This diagnostic report is what a teacher would be most interested in for helping individual students and for making instructional and course design decisions. This would also be most useful for students interested in continuous improvement. If these individual sLO attainment values could then be averaged up to the GLO level for a higher-level view of how the students as a group are achieving, this would be helpful for making instructional and course redesign decisions for continuous improvement and for reporting at the department and program levels. These GLO attainment averages could then be averaged to

the Goal level for reporting to the chair or dean and for linking to department Goals and program Goals and then linking from program Goals to institutional Goals.

Unless you have a very small class, you would need a computer program to calculate the individual student attainment values. Even if individual outcomes could be calculated, in the typical classes of 25 or 30 students it would be a herculean task to provide individualized instruction based on the individualized outcome attainment data. In large classes, such as those with 100-plus students, this individualization would be impossible without some type of computer program that could analyze the data, give individualized instruction, reassess for progress, and then produce instant reports.

Fortunately, programs have become and are becoming available that can provide student-level outcome attainment as well as tag outcome codes to scores so that outcome attainment at all levels can be reported. These outcome attainment values provide valuable information for making instructional and course redesign decisions and for providing formative information to students.

This chapter shows how to calculate the degree of SLO attainment at the class level, and chapter 9 will show how the course-level Goal attainment can be mapped up to the institutional levels; mapping in the form of tagging is what can be input into computer programs to calculate and report at all levels. More will be said about these programs at the end of chapter 9.

Test-Item Validity

Test-item validity is an integral part of the three-level Goal-attainment reporting process. In order to produce test scores that are valid for their intended use and purpose, the test items must have a high degree of validity. In other words, if there are flawed items on your test, then what the test is measuring will lack validity. Flawed MC items can be up to 15 percentage points more difficult than items that conform to recommended item-writing guidelines when testing the same content, and can have median passing scores that are 3.5 percentage points lower for flawed items compared to items that follow the guidelines (Downing, 2005).

The first piece of item validity evidence is that the items match the outcomes they are meant to test. As has been shown in previous chapters, this matching is done at the sLO level. If you want test results from an outcome-based assessment that are valid for their intended use and purpose, then you need to be able to show that your test items are testing what the outcomes state.

The second piece of item validity evidence is that the item-writing guidelines in chapters 4 and 5 are followed. Following the guidelines helps to produce items that function well statistically and thus reduce test score error.

The third piece of validity evidence is item anaysis, which based on how the item functions statistically. An item analysis provides the percentage or proportion of students choosing each answer choice plus information on how well each answer choice discriminated between high-scoring students who are expected to choose the correct answer and low-scoring students who are expected not to choose the correct answer.

Basic Item-Analysis Statistics

Table 8.1 introduces you to some basic item-analysis statistics. Statistics for two items are shown. For each item, column 2 shows the answer choices. Column 3 shows the proportion of students who chose each answer choice. Column 4 shows the proportion of the lowest scoring 27% of students who chose each answer choice, and column 5 shows the proportion of the highest scoring 27% of students who chose each answer choice. For item number 4, the items discriminated well between the lowest scoring students who should have missed the item, and the highest scoring students who should have gotten the item correct, with proportions of .50 and .91, respectively. It can be concluded that Item Number 4 is functioning well.

Item number 5, however, has problems and can be considered to be a flawed item. Evidence for this

TABLE 8.1: Basic Item-Analysis Statistics

Item Number	Answer Choices	Proportion Chosen	Low 27%	High 27%
4	A*	.73	.50	.91
	B	.02	.06	.00
	C	.12	.23	.04
	D	.13	.21	.05
Item Number	Answer Choices	Proportion Chosen	Low 27%	High 27%
5	A	.07	.09	.05
	B	.22	.26	.18
	C	.49	.49	.45
	D*	.21	.14	.32

Note. *indicates correct answer

decision is that the proportion of students who chose answer choice C (an incorrect answer) is much higher than the proportion of students who chose answer choice D (the correct answer). Of course, it could be that the correct answer choice was supposed to be C, and thus the correct item is miskeyed, but even if that was the case, choice C has problems because, as indicated by columns 4 and 5, it does not discriminate well between the low-scoring and high-scoring student groups. The first step to fix item number 5 would be to see what item-writing guidelines were violated.

Item-Analysis Report for MC Items

Figure 8.1 shows an example of a more complete item-analysis report for four MC items. The text boxes describe what the values in each column indicate. Column 2 shows that item number 4 is the most difficult item, with a low proportion correct value of .18, and needs to be considered a flawed item. Item number 2 is the least difficult item, with 86% of the students choosing the correct answer, and it is likely an item designated as low difficulty on the test blueprint.

To examine the information in Figure 8.1 more closely, let's use item number 1 as an example. In column 2, you can see that option C is the correct answer because it is marked by an asterisk, and the total proportion of students endorsing option C (.61) is the same value as the *proportion correct* value in column 2. Now let's see how well this item discriminated between the lowest scoring students and the highest scoring students. In other words, did the highest scoring students who are expected to choose the correct answer do so, and did the lowest scoring students who are expected to not choose the correct answer do so?

In column 8 we can see that .86 of the highest scoring students chose C, and in column 7, .35 of the lowest scoring students chose C. The difference between these values gives the *discrimination index* value of .51 in column 3, and indicates that the items differentiated well between high-scoring and low-scoring students (generally an acceptable value is .30 and up). In other words, you would expect more high-scoring students to choose the correct answer (C) than low-scoring students.

The *point-biserial* value in column 4, which is the correlation between the proportion of students who endorsed the correct answer choice and the whole-test mean score for those students, is also above .30, which is acceptable and what you would expect with an acceptable *discrimination index*. The point-biserial value is the second indicator that the item discriminated well between low- and high-scoring students.

In column 8 we can see that the options that were the incorrect answers have negative point-biserial correlations, meaning that more low-scoring students than high-scoring students chose these options, which is what would be expected. Only the correct answer option should have a positive point biserial.

When the number of students choosing the correct answer option is very high or very low, the discrimination index and the point biserial for the correct answer will lose some of their usefulness, because they will typically be unacceptably low, but this is only because the way they are calculated is affected by the extremely high or low correct-answer values. This effect can be seen in items number 2 and number 3 where the point biserials are smaller.

There are scenarios other than what is shown in Figure 8.1, but what is shown and explained is most of what you will need to make decisions about how your test items function and what action you may want to take. Keep in mind that you, as the outcome and item writer, will need to make decisions about an item based on what you intended in your outcome statement, how the outcome was taught, and how you expected the item to function when you wrote it.

Why Only Three Options Are Needed

Before we leave the topic of item analysis for multiple-choice items, let's look at Table 8.2, which shows only four of the columns from Figure 8.1. Note that contrary to the recommendation and research evidence provided in chapter 4 that only three answer choices (options) are needed, Table 8.2 shows the four items from Figure 8.1 with the four options for each item. The purpose of this is to demonstrate that a fourth option contributes very little statistically for making decisions about what the test item is measuring. Note in column 4 of Table 8.2 that each item has one proportion endorsing value that is very low. These low-value answer options are not of much use for making a decision about how the items functioned and therefore are not needed.

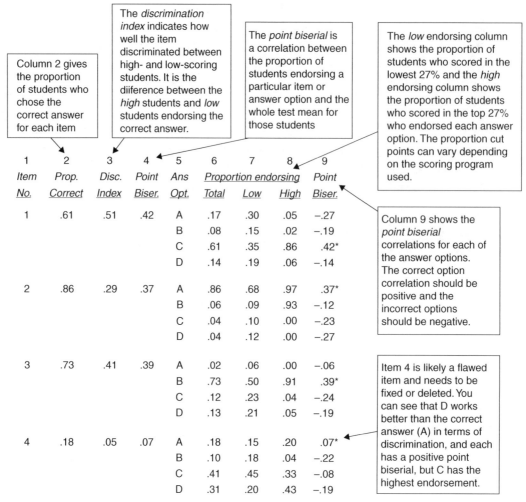

Column 2 gives the proportion of students who chose the correct answer for each item

The *discrimination index* indicates how well the item discriminated between high- and low-scoring students. It is the diiference between the *high* students and *low* students endorsing the correct answer.

The *point biserial* is a correlation between the proportion of students endorsing a particular item or answer option and the whole test mean for those students

The *low* endorsing column shows the proportion of students who scored in the lowest 27% and the *high* endorsing column shows the proportion of students who scored in the top 27% who endorsed each answer option. The proportion cut points can vary depending on the scoring program used.

Column 9 shows the *point biserial* correlations for each of the answer options. The correct option correlation should be positive and the incorrect options should be negative.

Item 4 is likely a flawed item and needs to be fixed or deleted. You can see that D works better than the correct answer (A) in terms of discrimination, and each has a positive point biserial, but C has the highest endorsement.

1	2	3	4	5	6	7	8	9
Item No.	Prop. Correct	Disc. Index	Point Biser.	Ans Opt.	Proportion endorsing Total	Low	High	Point Biser.
1	.61	.51	.42	A	.17	.30	.05	−.27
				B	.08	.15	.02	−.19
				C	.61	.35	.86	.42*
				D	.14	.19	.06	−.14
2	.86	.29	.37	A	.86	.68	.97	.37*
				B	.06	.09	.93	−.12
				C	.04	.10	.00	−.23
				D	.04	.12	.00	−.27
3	.73	.41	.39	A	.02	.06	.00	−.06
				B	.73	.50	.91	.39*
				C	.12	.23	.04	−.24
				D	.13	.21	.05	−.19
4	.18	.05	.07	A	.18	.15	.20	.07*
				B	.10	.18	.04	−.22
				C	.41	.45	.33	−.08
				D	.31	.20	.43	−.19

FIGURE 8.1: Item-Analysis Report

This low-value fourth option would be a third distractor, and it usually requires the most labor to create since you already created two distractors that are plausible, and coming up with a third plausible option is usually very difficult and, as the proportions in column 4 show, not very productive. Obviously the students figured out that it was not very plausible because only a few chose it. In Table 8.2 you can see by the boldfaced numbers that only three options, as stated in chapter 4, are needed for good measurement. You will save valuable item-writing time by electing a three-option (two-distractor) item format.

For mathematics and some of the sciences, it is much easier to come up with the third distractor, due to the nature of the content, but typically one of the options will still have a very low proportion of endorsement. This is not to say that there could not be a reason to have a fourth or fifth option due to the nature of the content, but if the item analysis shows that the fourth or fifth option is not contributing enough information for decision-making, then it likely is not needed.

In addition to the time saved by having to write only three options, there is another advantage. You can add more items to the test form because students will spend less time per item. The more well-constructed items that you have on a test form, the higher the reliability of the test score, and test-score reliability is valuable validity evidence for the interpretation and use of the test score for its intended purpose.

Item-Response Analysis for CR Items

Rubric scores of a student's CR can be used to determine how the CR item functioned. Table 8.3 shows the scores for each student in a class on the outcomes

Item No.	Proportion Correct	Answer Option	Proportion Endorsing
1	.61	A	.17
		B	**.08**
		C	.61*
		D	.14
2	.49	A	**.07**
		B	.22
		C	.49*
		D	.21
3	.73	A	.73*
		B	**.02**
		C	.12
		D	.13
4	.82	A	**.02**
		B	.82*
		C	.05
		D	.10

TABLE 8.2: Statistically Why Only Three Options Are Needed

Note. * indicates correct answer

with decision-making, outcome attainment values for compensatory and conjunctive scoring (see chapter 6) are also shown. To analyze the item, three questions to ask are:

1. Do the average scores for each outcome make sense in terms of the intent and difficulty of the outcome being measured? If not, then you may need to revisit your outcome statement or how the question was asked in relation to the prompt, or both.
2. Do the student responses appear to reflect what was taught in terms of the outcomes they are measuring? If not, then you may need to revisit your instruction.
3. Did the prompt and the question seem to work? That is, did they produce a high degree of response? If not, then you may need to revisit your prompt, question, or both, plus any instructions that were provided.

Table 8.4 presents summary data for a chemistry course assignment in which students were asked to construct a response in writing. The students were expected to address the outcome content (shown in the first column) plus demonstrate that they have writing skills (shown in the second column). Note that the conjunctive scores are lower than the compensatory scores. This is almost always the case because conjunctive scoring requires a passing score minimum for all outcomes, such as all scores must be at least 3 on the scoring scale.

Calculating Outcome Attainment Values

A key point in this chapter is that in order to have valid information to use and to report about how well your students achieved the SLOs for your course, you must have test scores that are valid to a high degree, and you must have a way to calculate the results in terms of group (i.e., class) attainment. To accomplish this, we turn again to the three-level model.

Figure 8.2 shows the structure for calculating the attainment values, starting with the proportion of students who got the items correct for each set of items that measure a particular sLO. For demonstration purposes, it is easiest to start with results from an MC test, so this is what is shown in the diagram. The following instructions are to help you think through what is

that were measured on a scoring rubric. The outcomes measured are in the third row and are the same as shown in the analytic scoring rubric presented in chapter 6 (see Table 6.3). The first two rows in Table 8.3 are added to emphasize that the outcomes can be at the GLO or sLO level, as explained in chapter 6.

To determine an estimate on how the item (composed of the instructions, prompt, and question) functioned, you need to compute the mean of the individual scores for each outcome as shown in the bottom rows of Table 8.3. A four-point scale of 1 to 4 was used to score each outcome. Note that 40 students were measured, but scores for students 13 through 37 are not shown in order to reduce the size of the table. As can be seen, the *logic* outcome has a mean of 1.98, which is considerably lower than the other outcome means. This lower score may indicate that this is simply a difficult outcome, or it may indicate that the instructions were not clear, or that the prompt did not accommodate the expected outcome, or that there was not sufficient instruction on logic. To help

TABLE 8.3: Item Analysis for CR Scores

GLO	1.1	1.2	1.3	1.4	
sLO	1.1.1	1.1.2	1.1.3	1.1.4	
Student	Clarity	Structure	Logic	Reference Evidence	Content Total
1	3	2	2	1	8
2	3	3	3	3	12
3	4	3	2	3	12
4	3	3	2	2	10
5	2	2	1	2	7
6	2	2	3	3	10
7	4	3	2	3	12
8	4	4	3	3	14
9	3	4	2	4	13
10	3	2	1	3	9
11	2	3	2	1	8
12	2	2	1	2	7
...	...	...	...	...	...
38	2	3	2	2	9
39	1	2	1	1	5
40	2	3	3	3	11
Mean	2.65	2.75	1.98	2.38	10.05
Comp.	.66	.69	.50	.60	.63
Conj.	.52	.56	.38	.39	.46

shown in the diagram. The values can be easily calculated using an Excel spreadsheet as shown in Table 8.5. The instructions also apply to the Excel spreadsheet.

sLO Attainment

The first column in Figure 8.2 shows that there are 20 items on the test. You can see that each item is linked to an sLO, and each sLO is linked to a GLO, and each GLO is linked to the Goal. In other words, this is the three-level model you are already familiar with. You can see that items 1 through 4 measure sLO 1.1.1, and sLO 1.1.1 is linked to GLO 1.1, which is linked to Goal 1. The four item proportions average to .80, so .80 is the Goal attainment for sLO 1.1.1. We can say

that the class as a whole attained .80 (or 80%) of sLO 1.1.1.

Items 5 through 7 are linked to sLO 1.1.2, and the average of these four proportions is .74. Thus, the attainment of sLO 1.1.2 for the class is .74. This sLO information can be used to make instructional and redesign decisions. You can see that the attainment value of .74 for 1.1.2 is lower than the other sLOs, but not significantly. However, item 5 is pulling the sLO average down for sLO 1.1.2 and may warrant a review in terms of possible flaws and instructional time spent on the sLO. Now, if item 5 had a value of .48, then it would be considered flawed because when an item is below .50, a conclusion is that the item is flawed.

TABLE 8.4: Summary Item Analysis for CR Scores									
Outcome (sLO or GLO) 1. Correct chemical formula was identified. 2. Correct symbols were used. 3. Two possible results from reactants were identified. 4. Description of reaction was accurate.					*Quality of Writing (sLO or GLO)* 1. Paper was logically structured and easy to read. 2. Description of results was clearly stated and to the point. 3. Grammar and spelling were correct.				
	1. Formula	*2. Symbols*	*3. Reactants*	*4. Reaction*	*Sub-total*	*1. Structure*	*2. Clear*	*3. Grammar, Spelling*	*Sub-total*
Mean	3.30	3.10	2.25	2.75	2.85	3.60	3.24	2.55	3.31
Comp	.85	.75	.68	.68	.74	.88	.75	.80	.81
Conj	.62	.66	.58	.39	.56	.75	.65	.68	.69

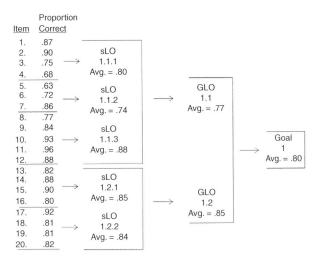

FIGURE 8.2: Calculating Outcome Attainment Values

The typical reasons for low sLO values are that the outcome is just very difficult to attain and needs to be reevaluated, or the instruction for the sLO needs to be modified, or one or more of the items for the sLO are flawed to some degree and need to be fixed or replaced.

GLO Attainment

As was stated, the sLO level is what instructors use for instructional and course redesign decisions. The GLO level is useful for reporting at the department (and possibly at the degree program) level. So let's see now how the GLO attainment value is calculated.

Note in the diagram that the first three sLOs link to GLO 1.1, and GLO 1.1 links to Goal 1. Because there are four items used for sLO 1.1.1, three items used for sLO 1.1.2, and five items for sLO 1.1.3, we don't have equal numbers of items per sLO, so it is necessary to do a weighted average of the three sLO attainment values to calculate the attainment value for GLO 1.1.

The easiest way to do this weighting is simply to add up all the proportions for items 1 through 12 and divide by 12, and you will get the weighted average attainment value of .77 for GLO 1.1. The value shown has been rounded from a number with at least three decimal places.

TABLE 8.5: Spreadsheet With Outcome Attainment Values

Item No.	Percent (%)	sLO	GLO	Goal	Item Difficulty
1	87	1.1.1	1.1	1	L
2	91	1.1.1	1.1	1	M
3	91	1.1.1	1.1	1	L
4	96	1.1.1	1.1	1	L
		91			
43	83	1.1.2	1.1	1	M
7	48	1.1.2	1.1	1	H
9	74	1.1.2	1.1	1	H
		68	**81**		
6	72	1.2.1	1.2	1	M
42	91	1.2.1	1.2	1	L
49	41	1.2.1	1.2	1	H
		68			
53	81	1.2.2	1.2	1	M
54	87	1.2.2	1.2	1	M
55	91	1.2.2	1.2	1	L
56	91	1.2.2	1.2	1	L
		88	**79**	**80**	
5	41	2.1.1	2.1	2	M
31	63	2.1.1	2.1	2	M
36	74	2.1.1	2.1	2	M
37	57	2.1.1	2.1	2	H
		59			
38	52	2.1.2	2.1	2	M
39	89	2.1.2	2.1	2	L
40	72	2.1.2	2.1	2	M
		71	**64**	**64**	

To calculate the attainment value for GLO 1.2 (linked to sLOs 1.2.1 and 1.2.2), you would add the percentages for items 13 through 20 and divide by 8 (same procedure as for GLO 1.1). Or, in this case, because there are four items each for sLOs 1.2.1 and 1.2.2 (i.e., equal), you could divide the two sLO values by 2. I recommend that for consistency you always do the sum of the items and divide by the number of items as done for GLO 1.1.

Goal Attainment

Now we come to the Goal attainment value for Goal 1, which of course is linked to GLO 1.1 and GLO 1.2. To get the weighted Goal attainment value for

Goal 1, total the percentages for items 1 through 20 and divide by 20.

Using a Spreadsheet to Record and Calculate Attainment Values

Very little math is required for calculating outcome attainment values. To make it easy, you can enter the values in an Excel spreadsheet. You can highlight each set of numbers you are working with and click on the sigma sign (Σ) in the icons, and then click on *Average*. The average values will be provided at the bottom of the set of numbers and with as many decimal places as you require.

Table 8.5 shows an example of how you can record all the data at once for calculating the attainment values. Notice in the table that the first set of items that measure sLO 1.1.1 are in sequential order. The second set of items that measure sLO 1.1.2 are not in sequential order because the items that measure the sLO are spread throughout the test form. In either case the steps to calculate the outcome attainment are the same. What is important is that the items are aligned to the correct sLO.

The boldfaced numbers in the sLO column are the averages of the item percentages for each set of items that were used to measure the sLO. The boldfaced numbers in the GLO column are the weighted averages for all the sLOs under that particular GLO. As was stated previously, the easiest way to calculate a weighted GLO outcome attainment value is to select

all of the item percentages that are associated with the GLO and calculate their average, and this value will be the weighted GLO value.

The boldfaced numbers in the Goal column are the weighted averages of the particular GLOs linked to the Goal. The easiest way to calculate a weighted Goal outcome is to select all of the item percentages that are associated with the GLO and calculate their average, and this value will be the weighted Goal value.

In the last column of the example are the difficulty levels for each item based on the percentage correct values in the second column. You estimated these values on your ORM (chapter 3), but now they can be more accurate because they are based on actual percentages from the test administration. At this time you could make corrections on your ORM. Remember, the ORM is a worksheet for tracking and aligning items with outcomes, including their estimated difficulty based on percentage correct values (also referred to as *difficulty* values or *p*-values).

Outcome Attainment Summary Reports

Tables 8.6 and 8.7 show useful ways to summarize and report your outcome attainment values. This information can be copied directly from the spreadsheet in Table 8.5. Table 8.6 shows the Goal, GLO, and sLO structure, but the focus is on the sLO attainment value and the particular items and the percentages correct that were used to calculate the sLO attainment value. Table 8.7 is a summary of attainment at each of the

	TABLE 8.6: Reporting sLO Outcome Attainment Values				
Goal	*GLO*	*sLO*	*Item Number*	*Percent (%) Correct*	*sLO Attainment*
1	1.1	1.1.1	1	99	1.1.1 85
1	1.1	1.1.1	2	93	
1	1.1	1.1.1	3	57	
1	1.1	1.1.1	4	89	
2	2.1	2.1.1	5	44	2.1.1 86
2	2.1	2.1.1	6	73	
2	2.1	2.1.1	7	82	
2	2.1	2.1.1	8	74	

TABLE 8.7: Summary Report of Goal, GLO, and sLO Attainment

Goal	GLO	sLO	Attainment (%)
1			81
	1.1		83
		1.1.1	**85**
2			75
	2.1		80
		2.1.1	**86**

TABLE 8.8: Calculating Attainment for Written-Response Rubric Scores

GLO	Students						Proportion of students receiving 3 or 4 points
	1	2	3	4	5	etc.	
1.1 Clarity of position statement	2	3	4	3	2		.80
1.2 Structure of the argument	3	3	3	4	2		.60
1.3 Logic of the argument	2	4	4	2	1		.50
1.4 Tone of response	3	2	3	2	1		.50
1.5 References and supporting evidence	3	4	1	2	1		.30

three levels. Note that the boldface sLO attainment values for 1.1.1 and 2.1.1 in Table 8.7 are the same values that are in the last column of Table 8.6.

These tables can be produced using Word or Excel, but they can also be produced using the outcome attainment calculator on my website (www .outcomesassessment.tools). Instructions are provided and show that when you enter the data in columns 3 through 5 of Table 8.6 you can produce the entire table with one click. With another click you can download the table as an Excel spreadsheet. With another click you can produce the summary table shown in Table 8.7. And with one more click you can download the table to an Excel spreadsheet.

Attainment Values for Written-Response Scores

As stated in chapter 5, written-response (constructed) test items that are designed to measure

SLOs are scored with analytic scoring rubrics and are usually measured at the GLO level, but they can also be measured at the sLO level depending on how broad or specific the content is. The sLO content is typically addressed to some degree in the cells for each GLO row when the GLO level is being scored. The analytic scoring rubric in chapter 6 (see Table 6.3) listed GLOs in the left-hand column, and the cells in each row contained descriptions of what was being measured.

The question then becomes: How can the rubric scores be incorporated into the Goal-attainment model? Table 8.8 provides the answer. In the left-hand column are the GLOs that are being scored. The scores received by each student on the GLOs are shown in the *Students* column under the student numbers (only students 1–5 are shown). In this example, we will say that a minimum score of 3 on the rubric scale is needed to be *proficient*. In other words, we are using conjunctive scoring. The proportions could also be average score proportions if a compensatory scoring was used. For the conjunctive scoring, the proportions of scores of 3 and 4 for each GLO are used to compute the attainment values for each GLO. Because these constructed-response GLOs are aligned with the same GLOs and sLOs as the MC test items, they can be considered an equivalent measure or co-measure to the MC outcome attainment values. More will be said about how to calculate combined attainment values in the next section.

Averaging Rubric Attainment Values with MC Values

If it can be determined that the constructed-response items are measuring the same outcomes as

the MC items, it makes sense to average the values as a measure that represents both assessment formats. Table 8.9 is an example of averaging the attainment values plus averaging up to the Goal level.

Reporting Goal Attainment

Table 8.10 shows the attainment values calculated for the GLO and Goal levels for a particular course. The GLO columns of the report would be of interest to chairs and departments as an executive summary of the degree to which your students attained the expected outcomes. The Goal-level sections of the report would be of interest to deans for application to

TABLE 8.9: Averaging Rubric Attainment Values with MC Attainment Values

GLO	MC Item Attainment Values	CR Item Attainment Values	Average of MC + CR Attainment	Goals	Goal Attainment
1.1	.80	.60	.70		
1.2	.75	.85	.80	1	.78
1.3	.90	.80	.85		
2.1	.65	.85	.75		
2.2	.70	.70	.70	2	.75
2.3	.80	.65	.73		
2.4	.85	.80	.83		

TABLE 8.10: Report of GLO and Goal Attainment for a Course

A Particular Course			
GLO	Attainment	Goal	Attainment
1.1	.81		
1.2	.79	1	.80
1.3	.91		
2.1	.60		
2.2	.65	2	.70
2.3	.79		
3.1	.83	3	.80
3.2	.78		

degree program SLOs. Reporting outcome attainment values satisfies accreditation agency requirements for a measure of student learning that relates directly to SLOs (grades are not acceptable).

Calculating Outcome Attainment From Various Sources

It is not uncommon to measure particular SLOs with different assessment formats and from different sources. The sources could be SR items, such as MC and matching, or CR, such as a written response, performance, and product. Other sources could be observations, surveys, individual projects, and team projects. As long as a score related to the sLO or GLO levels can be obtained, then a measure of the students' attainment of the outcome at the group level (course, section, or other type of group) can be calculated.

It would, of course, be ideal to also be able to report to the student how well the student did on each item

and sLO, but, as was mentioned earlier, unless the group is relatively small, reporting at the student level without technology support would be too labor intensive to do. Fortunately, computer programs have become available that allow tagging items to outcome statements and automatically provide outcome attainment values at the individual student level as well as the sLO, GLO, and Goal levels. More will be said about such programs at the end of chapter 9.

For now, let's consider how outcome attainment values from different sources can be averaged to provide one overall attainment value. Tables 8.11 and 8.12 show outcome attainment values obtained from three sources. All three sources were designed to obtain a measure of the student's ability to think critically. Source 1 is an MC test in which specific items were identified as measuring CT. Source 2 is a vignette, designed to specifically measure CT either as related to specific course content or CT in general using MC items (a written response to the vignette would also have been a source). Source 3 is a written response scored with a rubric designed to measure CT.

TABLE 8.11: Calculating CT Outcome Attainment From Different Sources With Equal Weighting

Source 1		Source 2		Source 3		Equal Value Weighted Averages			
Using course content MC items with one or more items identified as CT items, or a specific set of items designed to measure CT.		Using a vignette with MC items to measure CT within course content or to measure CT in general.		Using a written response item scored with an sLO-level rubric designed to measure CT.		Average of All Three Formats	Average Format 1 Plus Format 2	Average Format 1 Plus Format 3	Average Format 2 Plus Format 3
Goal 1. Students will be able to think critically.						F1 = .33 F2 = .33 F3 = .33	F1 = .50 F2 = .50	F1 = .50 F3 = .50	F2 = .50 F3 = .50
Goal	1	83	1	75	1	73	77	79	52	50
GLO	1.1	87	1.1	73	1.1	77	79	80	55	50
sLO	1.1.1	98	1.1.1	80	1.1.1			89		
sLO	1.1.2	75	1.1.2	65	1.1.2			70		
GLO	1.2	79	1.2	76	1.2	73	76	78	51	50
sLO	1.2.1	78	1.2.1	88	1.2.1			83		
sLO	1.2.2	55	1.2.2	72	1.2.2			64		

Table 8.11 shows the averaged attainment values when the source values are equally weighted. As can be seen in the source 3 column, the rubric used for measuring the written response was designed for the GLO level, and thus there are no attainment values for the sLO level. As was stated in previous chapters, this does not mean that the sLO level was not taught; it only means that it wasn't practical or feasible to include the number of rows in the rubric that would be needed to accommodate the number of sLOs.

Table 8.12 shows the same SLO attainment values for the three sources as Table 8.11. However, the averaged values are calculated with unequal weights, as can be seen in the last four columns. The weighting is accomplished by multiplying the attainment value by the desired weight and summing the values. For example, the *Average of all three formats* column for the *Goal* row shows the averaged attainment value of 78. Using the attainment value for each of the Goal sources (83, 75, and 73, respectively), the formula for this attainment value is $(.50 \times 83) + (.20 \times 75)$

$+ (.30 \times 73) = 78$. This unequal weighting provides flexibility for accommodating any weights an instructor might require. It also has application for inclusion in the institutional-level reporting that is covered in chapter 9.

Measuring Outcome Attainment of Learning Activities

In addition to being able to evaluate a course with outcome attainment values and then make instructional and course design decisions, you can evaluate particular learning activities to determine how effective they were in helping students attain the learning outcomes associated with the activities. Figure 8.3 shows an example of the relationships among an instructional activity, the sLOs that are being measured in relation to the activity, and the outcome attainment values that show the degree to which students attained the expected outcomes.

TABLE 8.12: Calculating CT Attainment From Different Sources With Unequal Weighting

Source 1		*Source 2*		*Source 3*		*Unequal Value Weighted Averages*			
Using course content MC items with one or more items identified as CT items, or a specific set of items designed to measure CT.		Using a vignette with MC items to measure CT within course content or to measure CT in general.		Using a written response item scored with an sLO-level rubric designed to measure CT.		*Average of All Three Formats*	*Average Format 1 plus Format 2*	*Average Format 1 Plus Format 3*	*Average Format 2 Plus Format 3*
Goal 1. Students will be able to think critically.						F1 = .50 F2 = .20 F3 = .30	F1 = .70 F2 = .30	F1 = .40 F3 = .60	F2 = .30 F3 = .70
Goal	1	83	1	75	1	73	78	80	77	74
GLO	1.1	87	1.1	73	1.1	77	81	84	81	76
sLO	1.1.1	98	1.1.1	80	1.1.1			69		
sLO	1.1.2	75	1.1.2	65	1.1.2			53		
GLO	1.2	79	1.2	76	1.2	73	77	77	75	74
sLO	1.2.1	78	1.2.1	88	1.2.1			55		
sLO	1.2.2	55	1.2.2	72	1.2.2			39		

Figure 8.3 is typical of an outcome-based model because the activity in the example was designed to help students obtain high attainment of the three sLOs shown in the sLO table. It is important for the instructor to know the degree to which the activity was able to accomplish this goal. If attainment is very low, then the activity would appear not to be successful and therefore not worth repeating, and the instructor would have to determine whether any of the following actions should be taken:

Drop the activity.

Revise the activity for a better match to the outcome statements.

Revise instruction for a better match to the activity.

Revise the activity for a better match to instruction.

Revise the test items or scoring rubric used to measure the outcomes for a better match to the outcomes and instruction.

Looking at the outcome attainment values in Figure 8.3, let's consider outcome 1.3.2. It appears that the activity was successful for helping students do well on sLO 1.3.2, and there is no indication that any of the items that measure 1.3.2 may be flawed.

Next let's consider outcome 2.1.2. The attainment value of .53 for sLO 2.1.2 is very low because items

42 and 32 are very low. These low item values may indicate that the item should be reviewed for flaws since the general rule is that items under .50 likely are flawed (i.e., violate the item-writing guidelines or are statistically flawed), or it could be that the activity may need to be revised to better align instruction with the outcome and test items, or this is simply a difficult outcome to attain.

Now let's look at the attainment for sLO 1.2.3. We might decide that the sLO average of .69 is too low to be acceptable. However, we can see that the low proportion correct of .38 for item 4 indicates it is a flawed item, and if it is fixed, then the sLO average of .69 attainment could be considerably higher since the other three items have moderate to high attainment values. In terms of validity, we could conclude that item 4 lacks validity for use as a measure of sLO 1.2.3. Therefore, it should be deleted from scoring and grading, and the sLO 1.2.3 average score should be recalculated in order for the attainment value of sLO 1.2.3 to have a high degree of validity.

Reporting Attainment With Criterion Levels

At some point you likely will need to provide reports to your department chair or at the program level regarding how well your students have achieved success on the outcomes for your class. Outcome attainment values, derived from student performance on validated test items, are highly valid measures for

Goal: MARKETING AND GENDER STEREOTYPING
The purpose of this assignment is to examine the marketing of toys and sports equipment as well as advertising images of boys and girls in play and sports contexts. The focus will be on memory capabilities of adults compared to the memory capabilities of children. The class will be divided into three groups. Each group will be assigned a specific task to research and will post their findings online.

sLO	Description				Marketing Experiential Activity				
		Item $n = 10$	Item %	sLO	sLO AV	GLO	GLO AV		
1.2.3	Students will be able to detect diffrences between subcultural market segments' attitudes toward brands.	23	83	1.2.3		1.2			
		18	67	1.2.3		1.2			
		22	88	1.2.3		1.2			
1.3.2	Students will be able to detect diffrences between consumer subcultural market segments' attitudes toward brands.	**4**	**38**	1.2.3	69	1.2	na		
		13	98	1.3.2		1.3			
		14	86	1.3.2		1.3			
2.1.2	Students will be able to relate how self-identity may impact consumers on consumption choices.	16	85	1.3.2	**91**	1.3	na		
		42	56	2.1.2		2.1			
		32	**50**	2.1.2	**53**	2.1	na		

FIGURE 8.3. Outcome Attainment Applied to a Specific Learning Activity

reporting student achievement. Grades are not highly valid measures because they do not directly link to outcome statements. For this reason, outcome attainment measures are preferred and requested by accreditation organizations.

It is easy to argue that attainment values mapped from the course level to institutional level are valid at the institutional level because the values can be traced back to the test items used to calculate the outcome attainment at the course level. Chapter 9 will demonstrate how outcome attainment can be mapped to the program and institutional levels.

At the course level, outcome attainment values are useful and valid for evaluating your instructional model and for making decisions about course redesign. They are also useful for reporting at the department and college levels in terms of meeting outcomes and for setting improvement goals. Setting criterion levels as shown in Tables 8.13, 8.14, and 8.15 can provide summary statements such as the following:

The class as a whole met the criterion on four out of five SLOs.

The class met the criterion on both GLOs and the overall Goal.

An improvement goal is to raise the GLO criterion to .82.

Our improvement goal is to increase Goal 1 attainment by 3 points within one year.

Completing the Links

As stated previously, course Goals can be mapped to program Goals, and program-level Goals can be mapped to institutional Goals. Figure 8.4 provides an introduction to how the mapping structure works. The course Goals that link to the program Goals may come from several different courses; in the same manner, program Goals that link to institutional Goals may come from several different programs. It is not expected that all the Goals for each course will link to program Goals, nor that all program Goals will link to institutional Goals. Chapter 9 will show in more detail how this mapping process from course to program to institution works.

TABLE 8.13: Attainment Report With Criterion at the sLO Level			
sLO	*Attainment*	*Criterion*	*Difference*
Specific Outcome 1	.81	.80	+.01
Specific Outcome 2	.60	.70	-.10
Specific Outcome 3	.88	.80	+.08
Specific Outcome 4	.85	.80	+.05
Specific Outcome 5	.85	.80	+.05

TABLE 8.14: Attainment Report With Criterion at the GLO Level			
GLO	*Attainment*	*Criterion*	*Difference*
General Outcome 1	.81	.80	+.01
General Outcome 2	.85	.80	+.05

TABLE 8.15: Attainment Report With Criterion at the Goal Level

Goal	Attainment	Criterion	Difference
Goal 1	.83	.80	+.03

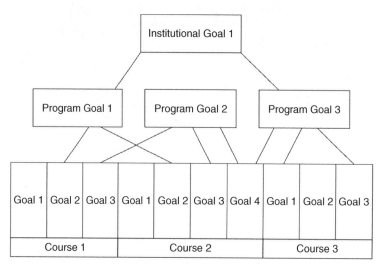

FIGURE 8.4: Linking From Course to Program to Institutional Goals

CHAPTER 9

Applying the Three-Level Model at the Institutional Level and Beyond

THE FOCUS OF THE first eight chapters of this book has been on the application of the three-level outcome-based model at the course (classroom) level. Now we are ready to move into the institutional level and beyond with the model. The last section in chapter 8 introduced the concept of linking outcome attainment information from the course level to the institutional level. In this chapter it will be demonstrated how this can be accomplished by mapping the course Goal-attainment values to institutional-level Goals plus how external Goal sources can be mapped in.

A condition for successful mapping is that the intent and wording of the institutional-level Goals have to match to a high degree the wording of the course-level Goals. An issue is that Goal statement alignments among departments, colleges, and the institutional levels are not always clear. However, with increasing pressure from accrediting and other educational organizations for outcome-based reporting, there have been increasing efforts to develop better alignments. Typically, it falls to the individual instructors and departments to write outcomes that align with the institutional-level Goals so that ultimately outcome attainment measures can be sent to the institutional folks so they can then report them to an accreditation organization.

There is no doubt that outcome-based assessment has become the norm at all levels of education. The Council for Higher Education Accreditation (CHEA) is a private, nonprofit organization that coordinates accreditation of its members, which includes more than 3,000 colleges and universities and over 60 national, regional, and specialized accreditors. CHEA holds

accrediting organizations responsible for "establishing clear expectations that institutions and programs will routinely define, collect, interpret, and use evidence of student learning outcomes," and states that "institutions and programs are responsible for establishing clear statements of student learning outcomes and for collecting, interpreting, and using evidence of student achievement" (CHEA, 2003).

Regional accreditation organizations use outcome-based language in their standards and guidelines. The Southern Association of Colleges and Schools Commission on Colleges (SACSCOC), one of the CHEA members, states in its Standard 3.3.1 that the institution "identifies expected outcomes, assesses the extent to which it achieves these outcomes, and provides evidence of improvement" (SACSCOC, 2012, p. 48). In 3.3.3.1 it states that educational programs are "to include student learning outcomes" (p. 48).

The Middle States Commissions on Higher Education (MSCHE), also a member of CHEA, requires in its *Standards for Accreditation and Requirements of Affiliation* (MSCHE, 2015) "clearly stated educational goals at the institution and degree/program levels" (p. 10) and assessments that evaluate the "extent of student achievement of institutional and degree/program goals" (p. 10).

National discipline-specific accreditation organizations have developed their own standards. For example, the Association to Advance Collegiate Schools of Business (AACSB), recognized by CHEA, requires business schools to have "processes for determining for each degree program learning goals that are relevant and appropriate" and "systems in place to assess whether learning goals have been met" (AACSB, 2013, p. 29).

The Accreditation Board of Engineering and Technology (ABET) is also an accrediting organization recognized by CHEA. ABET accredits postsecondary programs in applied science, computing, engineering, and engineering technology. ABET defines *Program Educational Objectives* as "what graduates are expected to attain within a few years of graduation," *Student Outcomes* as "what students are expected to know and be able to do by time of graduation," and *Performance Indicators* as "measurable statements identifying the performance required to meet the outcome" (ABET, 2011).

There is also a growing movement toward a competency approach for postsecondary educational certificates, badges, degrees, and programs that use an outcome-based model. In June 2015 the Council of Regional Accrediting Commission released a common framework for defining and approving *competence-based education programs* (Council of Regional Accrediting Commission, 2015). Western Governors University (WGU) has been a leader of the competency-based approach to awarding degrees and certificates. An article in *Inside Higher Ed* by Paul Fain (2013) reported that "competency-based education is spreading among community colleges, thanks to an assist from Western Governors University," supported by funding from the Bill and Melinda Gates Foundation and the U.S. Department of Labor. The article further stated that "competency-based education . . . ideally at least—more clearly describes what students know and can do than can conventional grades and transcripts" (Fain, 2013).

There are also large independent organizations that propose what students should be expected to know and do in order to obtain degrees from educational institutions. Because of their strong influence, it is reasonable that the learning outcomes proposed by these organizations may need to be addressed at the course level if the institution is making the outcomes part of the institutional learning Goals. Examples of how this can be accomplished will be provided later in this chapter. So the examples in this chapter will make more sense to readers who are not familiar with the organizations, the organizations are briefly explained here with references for those who want to do further study.

Let's talk about Tuning USA. Tuning encourages faculty members across insitutions to collaborate with one another to define outcomes for the attainment of degrees in specific disciplines. Any institution may use the outcome statements. Tuning was started in 2000 in Europe, and spread to other countries including the United States. Tuning USA has been involved in projects in several states that have developed outcomes for various disciplines. A PowerPoint presentation explaining Tuning can be found at www.google.com/?gws_rd=ssl#q=tuning+uSA+indiana+committee.

If you research Tuning USA, you will find many references to the Lumina Foundation, the National Institute for Learning Outcomes Assessment (NILOA), and the Degree Qualifications Profile (DQP). Lumina is a large private foundation focused "solely on increasing Americans' success in higher education," with a commitment to increase "the proportion of Americans with high-quality degrees, certificates and other credentials to 60 percent by 2025" (www.luminafoundation.org). NILOA "assists institutions and others in discovering and adopting promising practices in the assessment of college student learning outcomes" (www.learningoutcomesassessment.org/AboutUs.html).

Lumina publishes the DQP, which "provides a baseline set of reference points for what students should know and be able to do for the award of associate, bachelor's and master's degrees, regardless of their fields of study," and "describes what students should know and be able to do as they progress through progressive higher levels of postsecondary study" (NILOA, 2014). NILOA maintains the Lumina DQP website.

The DQP is of interest for this chapter because of its strong influence on what institutions may state in their institutional Goals and the degree to which there is alignment with DQP expected outcomes. A primary consideration is the fact that the DQP "invites and supports an allied process" with Tuning because Tuning encourages the development of disciplinary-level outcomes that can be used within the DQP. The three choices on the DQP home web page are "What is the DQP/Tuning process?"; "Why do we need the DQP and Tuning?"; and "How do we implement the DQP and Tuning?" (NILOA, 2014).

Also of interest for this chapter is the work of the Association of American Colleges and Universities (AAC&U). AAC&U was founded in 1915 and is a national association headquartered in Washington, DC. As stated on its website, the association is "concerned with the quality, vitality, and public standing of undergraduate liberal education. Its members are committed to extending the advantages of a liberal education to all students, regardless of academic specialization or intended career" (Schneider, 2016, p. 1). Currently, the organization comprises "accredited public and private colleges, community colleges, research universities, and comprehensive universities of every type and size." In 2005 the organization launched an initiative entitled Liberal Education and America's Promise (LEAP) to "promote the value of liberal education." Four broad Essential Learning Outcomes (ELOs) were developed, and to determine how well students attain the outcomes, AAC&U launched in 2007 the Valid Assessment of Learning in Undergraduate Education (VALUE), which provides rubrics for 15 specific areas of learning directly related to the LEAP ELOs. A sixteenth rubric was added in 2013. The rubrics are typically referred to as the AAC&U LEAP VALUE rubrics. Their use has increased each year. For a comprehensive history of the rubrics, see *Using the VALUE Rubrics for Improvement of Learning and Authentic Assessment* by T. L. Rhodes and A. Finley (2013).

A Census Approach to Obtaining Outcome Measures

All institutions, whether pre- or postsecondary, strive to obtain meaningful measures of the degree to which students attain the learning outcomes stated by the institution. Elementary and secondary institutions are required to give state-developed assessments to measure outcomes. Postsecondary institutions use nationally normed assessments and samples of student work, which are typically rescored and used to represent the attainment of particular institutional-level outcomes. An example of a sampling method used by many institutions is when student writing samples are collected from a particular or various disciplines, raters score the samples with a specified scoring rubric, and the aggregated result is then used to report institutional-level attainment of the students' written communications skills.

This book recommends a census approach that is based on student performance at the course level for calculating outcome attainment measures that can be mapped up to higher levels. It is important to understand that with the three-level model outcome attainment values for all levels are derived from item

percentage correct scores. Item scores are averaged to obtain sLO-level attainment, sLO-level attainment values are then averaged to calculate GLO-level attainment values, and GLO-level attainment values are then averaged to calculate Goal-level attainment values. This method is called a *census approach* because all students who took the assessments are represented, rather than just a sampling of the students. This method could also be called a *grassroots approach* since all evaluation and reporting starts with the assessment items and includes SR items, CR items (written, performance, and product), observations, surveys, and interviews, plus any other format that is used to gather information about student attainment of the outcomes.

Thus, no assessing/testing at the GLO and Goal levels is necessary in order to calculate their values. This makes the GLO and Goal levels *reporting* levels. Likewise, no assessing/testing, assuming there is good alignment, would be necessary at the unit, department, college, or institutional levels because these higher level attainment values would be calculated in a hierarchical manner from the course Goal-attainment values. This means that rather than having to sample student work and rescore or use external tests to obtain attainment information about the outcome expectations within the organization, the existing course-level values would be used for all calculations. This does not mean, however, that particular external assessments required by the institution, state, or accreditation organizations for particular reporting purposes could be eliminated, but the argument will be made in the following sections that a demonstration of outcome-statement alignment with external assessments could be a valid measure for reporting attainment of what is covered in the external assessments. Although all of these links may not be possible now, developing technologies are fast approaching analysis of large data sets; tracking individual student progress on outcome attainment; measuring attainment across courses and disciplines; providing valid measures of institutional Goals; dispensing instant feedback to students and teachers; and producing automatic, continuous, and cumulative reporting at all levels. The implications of this mapping and aggregation process in terms of valid measures and resource savings, in addition to improving student learning, are worth investigating. Now it is time to see how the three-level model can be expanded to and beyond the institutional level.

Three-Level Model Overview

Chapter 8 ended with a basic diagram of the three-level model shown in Figure 9.1. It is important to understand that all measurement of outcome attainment starts with how the students performed on the test items that are used to measure the sLOs. The sLO values are then used to calculate the outcome attainment at all other levels. This linkage is demonstrated in Figure 9.2 by including the links from items to sLO to GLO. The steps to keep in mind for calculating outcome attainment are as follows: (a) Item-correct values are used to calculate sLO attainment, (b) sLO values are then used to calculate course GLO attainment, (c) course GLO values are then used to calculate course Goal attainment, (d) course Goal-attainment values are then used to calculate program Goal attainment, and (e) program Goal attainment is then used to calculate institutional Goal attainment.

Calculating Outcome Attainment at the Program Level

After calculating the Goal-attainment values for a course or course section, the values can easily be used to calculate program-level Goal attainment, as shown in Figure 9.2. The assumption for this process is that particular course-level Goal statements match

(i.e., align with) particular program-level Goal statements in terms of the words used and the explicit or implied meaning and intent of the words in relation to the learning expectations. In other words, syntax (sentence structure), semantics (word meaning), and intent (purpose and objective) play a role in being able to say that the outcome statements are in alignment. Good alignment increases validity.

You may find that the GLO statements under a course Goal are more similar in wording and meaning to the program Goal statement than to the Goal statement and thus can add clarity and help in the process of making the connection between course Goal and program Goal. In other words, the GLO statements may help clarify and confirm that your decision about the match or alignment of the course Goal to the program Goal is valid.

Figure 9.2 shows three courses that have course Goals that match or align with program Goals. To demonstrate the calculation procedure, only the attainment values for the course Goals that match program Goal 2 are connected with lines. As can be seen in the second column of the program Goal table, the attainment values, when averaged, result in a .79 attainment value for program Goal 2. Since we are assuming a good fit of the course Goal statement wording to program Goal 2 wording, we can say with a high degree of confidence that the .79 value is a valid measure of the degree to which students in the program attained

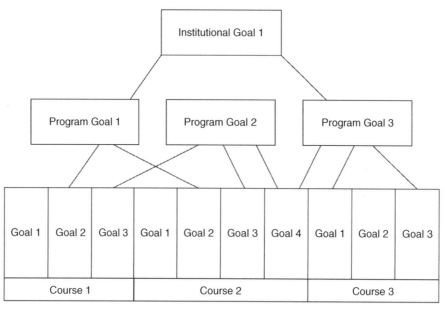

FIGURE 9.1: Three-Level Model Overview

the Goal, and it can be reported that 79% of program Goal 2 was attained.

As validity evidence, keep in mind that the .79 attainment of the program Goal can be tracked back through the course Goal attainment and down to the items on the assessment that were used to measure the attainment of the course sLOs. In other words, the process starts at the "grassroots" with the students' responses and includes all the students, making it a census measure without the need of additional program-level assessment. The program-level attainment values can then be reported to whomever requires a report.

Also note that the title for the program Goals table contains the words "or other." This is because the program Goals could be from any source, such as discipline accreditation goals from Tuning USA, or professional organization goals like AAC&U's LEAP Essential Learning Outcomes and VALUE rubrics. These connections will be discussed in later sections of this chapter.

Figure 9.3 shows a vertical display of how course Goals would map up to program Goals. The lines indicate which particular Goals from a particular course link to a particular program Goal. As the figure shows, Goals from different courses may link to a particular program Goal.

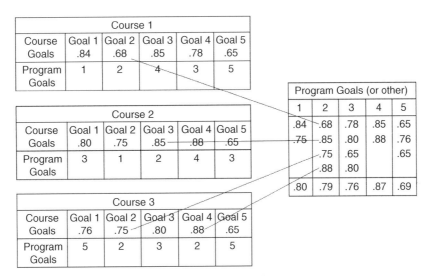

FIGURE 9.2: Calculating Program-Level Outcome Attainment From Course-Level Attainment

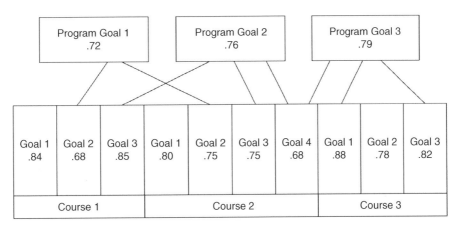

FIGURE 9.3: Vertical Display of Course to Program Connections

Calculating Outcome Attainment at the Institutional Level

The process for calculating institutional-level outcome attainment is identical to that for calculating program-level outcome attainment. The same reasoning applies except that, unlike the course level, which has a GLO level that might help with decision-making, the program level typically has only Goal-level statements. For our purposes, the same values from Figure 9.2 are used in Figure 9.4, and the table titles are changed to "Program" and "Institutional."

Figure 9.5 shows a vertical display of how program Goals would map up to institutional Goals. The values are the same as were used in Figure 9.3, but in this case the lines indicate which particular Goals from a particular program link to a particular institutional Goal. As the figure shows, Goals from different programs may link to a particular institutional Goal.

The Three-Level Model With Attainment Values

Now let's revisit the diagram shown previously as Figure 9.1 and add in the outcome attainment values, as shown in Figure 9.6. As can be seen, the course Goal outcome attainment values map up to all other

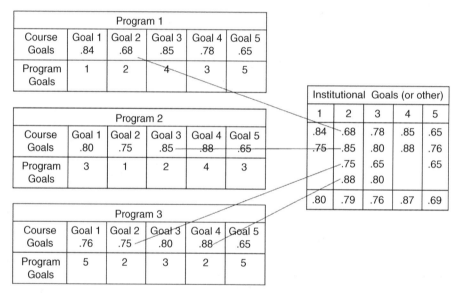

FIGURE 9.4: Calculating Institutional Attainment From Program Values

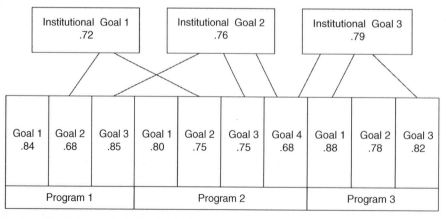

FIGURE 9.5: Vertical Display of the Program to Institution Connection

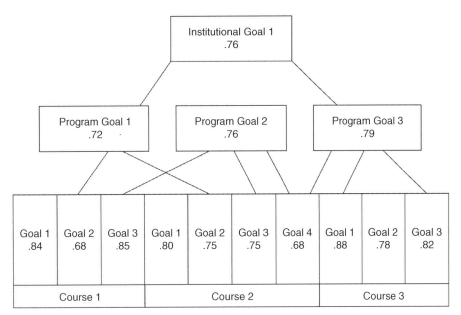

FIGURE 9.6: Three-Level Model Showing Outcome Attainment Values

levels and, as will be shown in the following sections, can also be used to map to discipline-accreditation organization goals and to goals from outside organizations that may be implemented by your institution.

Mapping Specific Course Content Attainment to the Institutional Level

Institutions have SLO goals for improvement of student learning as well as goals for program improvement, and academic degree programs strive to address both types of institutional Goals. To demonstrate how the three-level model figures into this scheme, Figure 9.7 shows institutional Goal 1 as a *learning Goal* that requires students to "think critically," and Institutional Goals 2 and 3 are *program Goals*. As would be expected, for Program A, there are also learning and program Goals, and the program *learning Goal* is that the student will be able to "think critically."

Program A, Goal 1 has an outcome attainment of .78 for the measure of CT. So why, you may be asking, does the institutional Goal 1 attainment value to which the program Goal maps have an attainment value of .82? The reason is that other academic programs also contribute to the attainment of institutional Goal 1, and their attainment values would have to be averaged in.

Figure 9.7 shows that each of the three core courses has learning Goals that required students to "think

critically," and it is their outcome attainment values that average up to .78 for the program Goal attainment. Note that the three courses are designated as *core courses*, but it could be that other noncore courses also required CT, in which case their attainment values would also be averaged in.

Keep in mind that this is still a census approach, since the outcome attainment values are coming from all the students in all the courses who were measured. The next section shows how the model can be used to incorporate external organization outcomes.

Mapping From Common Courses With Links to Outside Sources

In the previous example, the outcome attainment measures came from three core courses that had Goals that required the attainment of CT skills. The core courses could be from the same discipline or from different disciplines. Continuing to use CT as an example, Figure 9.8 demonstrates mapping from three chemistry courses to the degree program Goals for chemistry. In this example there are three learning Goals at the program level, but only program Goal 1 is *critical thinking*, and the attainment value is calculated from three chemistry courses. The average from the three courses can be reported as .75 attainment for program Goal 1. Remember that the attainment value at the course level is a census measure, and after

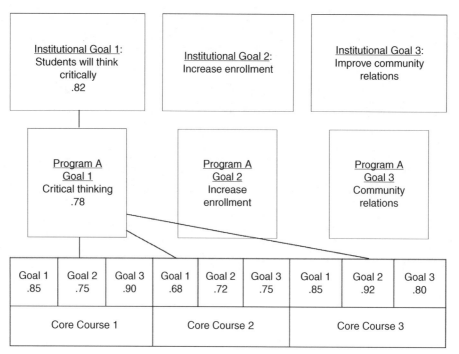

FIGURE 9.7: Specific Content From Course to Institution

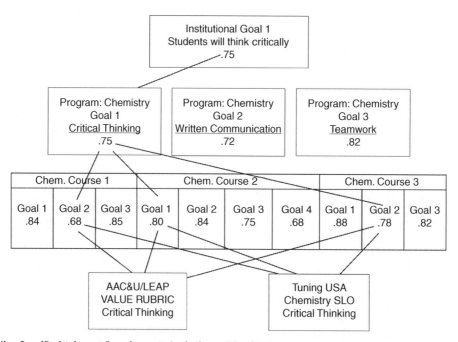

FIGURE 9.8: Discipline-Specific Attainment From Course to Institution and Outside Sources

attainment is calculated at the course level, no testing at the program level is required. The attainment values for program Goals 2 and 3 would be calculated from other chemistry course goals, although it would not be unusual for program Goal 2, *written communication*, and program Goal 3, *teamwork*, to be part of the same

instructional activity. For example, students could be asked to *demonstrate the ability to think critically in a written communication developed within a team.*

Additional links are made from the course level to the AAC&U VALUE rubric for *critical thinking* and to a Tuning USA outcome requiring *critical thinking*. This means that the wording and intent of the course-level outcome statement was a good match to the wording that addressed the Tuning USA outcome statements requiring students to be critical thinkers. It would not be unreasonable to use the course-level attainment as evidence that the outcomes recommended by the two organizations were being addressed.

Mapping From Different Disciplines With Links to Outside Sources

Figure 9.9 shows an extension of the model to include additional external organizations, each of which requires CT, and to demonstrate how the course-level Goal-attainment values can come from three different disciplines. The assumption is that there is similar wording regarding CT as an expected outcome within and among all the connections. The final institutional Goal-attainment value can then be utilized by institutional research, effectiveness, and assessment departments and reported to state and accreditation agencies. Colleges and academic departments can report the outcome attainment for their programs directly to the institutional departments. Discipline programs can report goal attainment directly to their professional accreditation organizations and can demonstrate how they have addressed the organization goals.

Program and Curriculum Mapping of Outcome Attainment

A common scheme for mapping program and curriculum expectations is to use some form of a table. When outcome attainment values can be calculated, the values can be used for the cells to provide an objective and usable measure. Table 9.1 provides an example of a way to use the attainment measures from the three-level model for reporting and decision-making. Other variables such as year, semester, department, and so forth could be accommodated with the spreadsheet format, but for learning outcome, the bottom line is always course evaluation and the degree to which students have attained the outcomes.

Concluding Comments

This book has presented a way to objectively and meaningfully assess student learning and evaluate course instruction by calculating, using, and reporting outcome attainment values. To get the most benefit from this process, you will need to link your outcomes and assessments to your instructional activities, and then use the assessment results to make instructional and course redesign decisions. If your instruction is linked to your outcomes and assessment, then the data you collect will have a high degree of validity for making these instructional

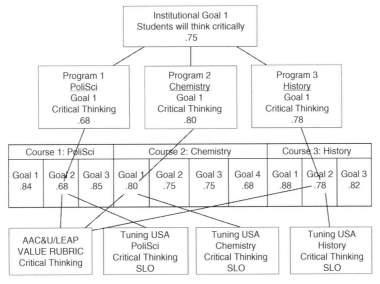

FIGURE 9.9: Different Disciplines' Outcome Attainment From Course to Institution and Outside Sources

TABLE 9.1: Spreadsheet Format for Mapping Course Goals to Program Goals

	Attain-ment	*Program Goal 1*	*Program Goal 2*	*Program Goal 3*	*Program Goal 4*	*Program Goal 5*
Course 1 Goal 1	.84					
Course 1 Goal 2	.68	.68				
Course 1 Goal 3	.85		.85			
Course 2 Goal 1	.80					
Course 2 Goal 2	.75	.75				
Course 2 Goal 3	.75		.75			
Course 2 Goal 4	.68		.68	.68		
Course 3 Goal 1	.68			.88		
Course 3 Goal 2	.88					
Course 3 Goal 3	.78			.82		
Program attainment		.72	.76	.79		

decisions, particularly in terms of continuous improvement.

The last pages of this book showed how Goal-attainment values can link to department, program, and institutional levels. Making these links helps with reporting student learning at these higher levels, but the attainment values at these higher levels tell very little about student-level learning; it is at the student and class level that assessment is most meaningful. As you get further removed from what you are actually trying to measure (i.e., student learning at the course level), usefulness of the data for enhancing student learning diminishes. It is necessary to report student learning at the department, program, and institutional levels, for various reasons, but if the student-level data used for this reporting is not valid information at the course level, then what is reported at these higher levels will lack validity for making meaningful decisions, which emphasizes again the value of the outcome-based assessment model presented in this book.

As was stated previously, the three-level model outcome attainment calculation and reporting works best when outcome attainment values can be automatically calculated and reported at all levels. As examples, I will share here a few of the programs that I have had personal experience with that provide the information needed for making outcome-based instructional and course-design decisions.

Learning management systems (LMSs) such as Blackboard allow tests to be developed and given within the program and provide response analysis and item-analysis data. Both SR and CR items can be written in Blackboard. Categories, including a Goal, a GLO, and an sLO designation, can be mapped to test items. The data reported are not always easy to retrieve in a format that is preferred by a three-level model user. Third-party products can be used that integrate with Blackboard to get the information you need in a format that you find most usable.

One of the products available today that addresses a highly usable reporting format and provides item analysis as well as analysis of student performance on learning outcomes linked to test items is Educational Assessments Corporation's (EAC) Visual Data. EAC Visual Data makes the process of mapping, collecting, analyzing, and reporting SLO data easy and intuitive. The EAC Visual Data interface integrates into an institution's LMS to efficiently analyze data and produce reports for a particular test and also for a common test administered across multiple courses and multiple sections. EAC Visual Data is capable of analyzing both SR data such as MC test and CR data from rubric-scored assignments such as essays. EAC will analyze SLOs tagged to test items if the tagging has been performed in either the LMS or the EAC environment. Data sources can be from tests taken in an LMS or from scanned bubble sheets.

EAC reports include student reports that show graphically item-response information such as correct and incorrect responses, the test question, and the outcome being measured and allow mapping of items to the sLO so students can also see their outcome attainment of the sLO. Instructor reports show individual student and group data at the Goal, GLO, and sLO levels in table and graphic formats. The reports are easy to access and are at an information level that is easy for teachers and students to digest.

A product that is well known for its online testing capabilities and that provides data and usable reports similar to what EAC produces plus more extensive information is ExamSoft. The program's data analysis and reporting includes tracking item and student performance over time as well as being able to tag categories and outcomes, such as the three-level model. The program provides question and assessment creation, produces question history reports, and integrates with LMS programs. Features include instant scoring and rescoring, student feedback reports, and detailed faculty reports for both SR and written-response assessments. ExamSoft states that it is the leading computer-based testing and analytics solution for law schools and bar examiners across the nation.

Since one issue all institutions have to consider is cost, my recommendation is that you do a careful needs assessment and determine what types and levels of data analysis you may need and what you can afford. You need to consider how much information you really need to achieve your goals and what type of reporting would be most beneficial for your needs: student and teacher, program-level administrator, institutional research and effectiveness director, institutional-level administrator, or any of the other myriad positions that are in the educational systems today. For three-level model users, the bottom line is always obtaining, using, and reporting valid outcome-based assessment information.

References

Accreditation Board of Engineering and Technology (ABET). (2011). *Accreditation criteria.* Retrieved from http://www.abet.org/accreditation/why-abet-accreditation-matters/a-valued-credential/

Adelman, C., Ewell, P., Gaston, P., & Schneider, C. (2014). *The degree qualifications profile.* Indianapolis, IN: Lumina Foundation. Retrieved from http://www.luminafoundation.org. and http://www.DegreeProfile.org

Airasian, P. W. (1991). *Classroom assessment.* New York, NY: McGraw-Hill.

American College Testing (ACT) (2008). *Collegiate Assessment of Academic Proficiency (CAAP).* Retrieved from http://www.act.org/content/act/en/products-and-services/act-collegiate-assessment-of-academic-proficiency/about-act-collegiate-assessment-of-academic-proficiency.html

Anderson, L. W., & Krathwohl, D. R. (Eds.). (2001). *A taxonomy for learning, teaching, and assessing: A revision of Bloom's taxonomy of educational objectives.* New York, NY: Addison Wesley Longman.

Association to Advance Collegiate Schools of Business (AACSB). (2013). *Eligibility procedures and accreditation standards for business accreditation.* Retrieved from http://www.aacsb.edu/accreditation/standards

Bloom, B. S. (1956). *Taxonomy of educational objectives: The classification of educational goals. Handbook I: Cognitive domain.* New York, NY: David McKay Company.

Council for Higher Education Accreditation (CHEA). (2003). *Statement of mutual responsibilities for student learning outcomes: Accreditation, institutions, and programs.* Washington, DC: CHEA Institute for Research and Study of Accreditation and Quality Assurance, Council for Higher Education Accreditation. Retrieved from http://www.chea.org

Council of Regional Accrediting Commission. (2015). *Regional accreditors announce common framework for defining and approving competency-based education programs* [Press release]. Retrieved from http://www.accjc.org/wp-content/uploads/2015/10/C-RAC_CBE_Statement_Press_Release_06_02_2015.pdf

Downing, S. M. (2005). The effects of violating standard item writing principles on tests and students: The consequences of using flawed test items on achievement examinations in medical education. *Advances in Health Sciences Education, 10,* 133–143.

Downing, S. M. (2006). Selected-response item formats in test development. In S. M. Downing & T. M. Haladyna (Eds.), *Handbook of test development.* Mahwah, NJ: Erlbaum.

Driscoll, A., & Wood, S. (2007). *Developing outcomes-based assessment for learner-centered education.* Sterling, VA: Stylus.

Ewell, P. (2001). *Accreditation and student learning outcomes: A point of departure.* Washington, DC: Council for Higher Education Accreditation. Retrieved from http://www.chea.org/award/StudentLearningOutcomes2001.pdf

Facione, P. A. (2016) *Using the holistic critical thinking scoring rubric to train the discover of evidence of critical thinking.* Insight Assessment, California Academic Press. Retrieved from www.insightassessment.com

Fain, P. (2013, November 19). Adding competency to community. *Inside Higher Ed.* Retrieved from https://www.insidehighered.com/news/2013/11/19/group-two-year-colleges-work-western-governors-university-try-competency-based

Finch, F. L. (Ed.). (1991). *Educational performance assessment.* Rolling Meadows, IL: Riverside.

Gronlund, N. E. (1995). *How to write and use instructional objectives.* Upper Saddle River, NJ: Prentice Hall.

Haladyna, T. M. (1997). *Writing test items to evaluate higher order thinking.* Boston, MA: Allyn & Bacon.

Haladyna, T. M. (1999). *Developing and validating multiple-choice test items* (2nd ed.). Mahwah, NJ: Erlbaum.

Haladyna, T. M., & Downing, S. M. (1993). How many options is enough for a multiple-choice test item? *Educational and Psychological Measurement, 53,* 999–1010.

Haladyna, T. M., & Downing, S. M. (2004). Construct-irrelevant variance in high-stakes testing. *Educational Measurement: Issues and Practice, 23*(1), 17–27.

Klein, S. P., Kuh, G., Chun, M., Hamilton, L., & Shavelson, R. (2005). An approach to measuring cognitive outcomes across higher education institutions. *Research in Higher Education, 46*(3), 251–276.

Linn, R. L., & Gronlund, N. E. (1995). *How to write and use instructional objectives* (5th ed.). Upper Saddle River, NJ: Prentice Hall.

Linn, R. L., & Gronlund, N. E. (2000). *Measurement and assessment in teaching* (8th ed.). Upper Saddle River, NJ: Prentice Hall.

Marzano, R. J., Pickering, D., & McTighe, J. (1993). *Assessing student outcomes: Performance assessment using the dimensions of learning model.* Alexandria, VA: Association for Supervision and Curriculum Development.

Middle States Commission on Higher Education (MSCHE). (2015). *Standards for accreditation and requirements of affiliation* (13th ed.). Philadelphia, PA: Author. Retrieved from http://www.msche.org/documents/RevisedStandardsFINAL.pdf

NILOA. (2014). Degree Qualifications Profile. Retrieved from www.degreeprofile.org

Osterlind, S. J. (1998). *Constructing test items: Multiple-choice, constructed-response, performance, and other formats.* Norwell, MA: Kluwer Academic.

OutcomesAssessmentTools (n.d.). Retrieved from http://www.outcomesassessment.tools/index.html

Paul, R. (1992). *Critical thinking: What every person needs to survive in a rapidly changing world* (2nd ed.). Santa Rosa, CA: The Foundation for Critical Thinking.

Popham, W. J. (2002). *Classroom assessment: What teachers need to know* (3rd ed.). Boston, MA: Allyn & Bacon.

Rhodes, T. L., & Finley, A. (2013). *Using the VALUE rubrics for improvement of learning and authentic assessment.* Washington, DC: Association of American Colleges and Universities (AAC&U).

Rodriguez, M. C. (2005). Three options are optimal for multiple-choice items: A meta-analysis of 80 years of research. *Educational Measurement: Issues and Practice, 24*(2), 3.

Schneider, C. G. (2016). *AAC&U president issues call to action on diversity, equity, and inclusion in wake of court decision on race-based admissions* [press release]. Association of American Colleges & Universities. Retrieved from http://www.aacu.org/press

Southern Association of Colleges and Schools Commission on Colleges (SACSCOC). (2012). *Resource manual for the principles of accreditation: Foundations for quality enhancement.* Decatur, GA: SACSCOC. Retrieved from http://www.sacscoc.org/pdf/Resource%20Manual.pdf

Statman, S. (1988). Ask a clear question and get a clear answer: An inquiry into the question/answer and sentence completion formats of multiple-choice items. *System, 16*(3), 367–376.

Turner, P. M., & Carriveau, R. S. (2010). *Next generation course redesign.* New York, NY: Peter Lang.

Willingham, D. T. (2007, Summer). Critical thinking: Why is it so hard to teach? *American Educator*, 8–19.

Index

AACSB. *See* Association to Advance Collegiate Schools of Business

AAC&U. *See* American Association of Colleges & Universities

Accreditation Board of Engineering and Technology (ABET), 86

accuracy, of interpretation, 21

affective domain, 2

all of the above, multiple-choice answer, 42

American Association of Colleges & Universities (AAC&U), 1, 68, 86–87, 89
  mapping and links with rubric of, 92–93

analysis, 9, 14
  test item, 21, 70–73

analytic rubric, with proficiency descriptors, 51–54

annotation, SLO of, 6

answer choices, multiple-choice, 40–43, 71–73
  student input on, 35

application
  apply category, 8, 34
  test question template with, 21

argumentation, in critical thinking, 14, 21

assessment, 86. See also outcome attainment values; Overall Assessment Plan; tests
  outcome-based, 2, 37–38, 81–82
  performance-based, 49–50, 59–60
  types, 2

Association to Advance Collegiate Schools of Business (AACSB), 85

attainment. See outcome attainment

Bloom, Benjamin, 7, 12, 32, 34–35

CAAP. See Collegiate Assessment of Academic Progress

California Critical Thinking Skills Test (CCTST), 58

categories. See cognitive categories

causation, test questions using, 22

CCTST. See California Critical Thinking Skills Test

census approach, 1, 87–88

change, test question on modify or, 24

CHEA. See Council for Higher Education Accreditation

chemistry course, 34

clarifying statements, 3–5

clues, in test items, 41, 42, 47, 48

cognitive categories, 7–10
  cognitive domain, 1–2
  taxonomy blueprint, 32, 34–35
  test question templates and, 19, 20

cognitive difficulty, 12, 34, 39
  designations, 27
  estimating, 31
  increasing, 19–20

Collegiate Assessment of Academic Progress (CAAP), 58

comparing and contrasting, 14, 51

compensatory scoring method, 52

comprehend/understand category, 8

conclusion, test questions using, 22

conflict, 25
  resolution, 16

conjunctive scoring, 52, 53

consequences, test questions using, 22

constructed-response (CR) items, 2, 11, 13, 17
  extended-response items, 48
  item-response analysis for, 72–73
  performance-based assessments and, 59–60
  rubrics, 51–55
  test blueprint with selected-response and, 31–33
  writing, 47–50

correct and proper way, test questions using, 22

correct answers, 42

correctness/representativeness, 22

Council for Higher Education Accreditation (CHEA), 85

Council of Regional Accrediting Commission, 86

courses
  course level connections, 84, 88, 89, 91
  mapping from common, 91–93
  test item writing for new or redesigned, 37

CR. See constructed-response

critical thinking (CT), 10, 57, 59–60, 80
  consequences idea in, 14
  data and, 14
  defining, 12–13

information dealt with in, 15–16
    measuring, 58, 65–66
    outcome statements, 13–16
    rationale, 15–16
    resolution stage in, 16
    suggestions and recommendations, 16
cut points, scoring using set, 54

Dash, Nicole, 6
decisions, test questions involving, 22–23
Degree Qualifications Profile (DQP), 1, 86
describing, 23
    explaining differentiated from, 19
descriptive scoring scale, 51–54
difficulty. See cognitive difficulty
discriminate
    discrimination index, 71
    test blueprint with recognize, identify and, 33, 34
distractors, answer choice, 41–42, 43
DQP. See Degree Qualifications Profile

Educational Assessments Corporation's (EAC) Visual
    Data, 94–95
effects, will happen, did happen, 23
ELOs. See essential learning outcomes
error
    measurement, 1
    scoring, 40
essential learning outcomes (ELOs), 87
evaluate, as cognitive category, 9–10
ExamSoft, 95
explaining
    describing differentiated from, 19
    test question on, 23
extended-response items, 48

fact vs. opinion, test question template on, 23
Fain, Paul, 86
fill in the blank items. See sentence-completion items
final cumulative exam, 27
Finley, A., 87
foils, 41

general learning outcome level (GLO), 5, 18, 31–34
    attainment report with criterion, 83
    calculating outcome attainment, 73–77
    number of test items per, 28
    verbs for writing, 10, 11
goal level, 3, 4–5, 75
    goal attainment reporting, 79
    institutional, 84, 88, 90, 91, 93
    linking course, program and institutional, 83–84

grading, test types and total points, 28
graduate level, test item difficulty for, 27

hierarchical model, for outcome statements, 11
higher order thinking, 12–13
history course, SLO structure for, 9
holistic rubric, 51, 52

identify, test blueprint with recognize and, 33, 34
information, in critical thinking, 15–16
institutional goal level, 84, 88, 90, 91, 93
instructions, test item, 17, 24, 25, 50
    on one-page test-item writing form, 39
intellectual abilities, measurement and, 2
interpretation
    accuracy of, 21
    interpret and apply, 34
item code, 39
item-response analysis, 72–73

justifying point of view, test question on, 23–24

knowledge category, 1, 7–8, 34

LEAP. See Liberal Education and America's Promise
learning management system (LMS), 38, 94, 95
learning outcomes. See student learning outcomes
Liberal Education and America's Promise (LEAP), 1, 68,
    87
literal level, 47
literature course, SLO example for, 7
LMS. See learning management system
logic, 15, 24
long responses, recording number of short and, 27–28

main idea, test question on purpose and, 25
mapping, 10–11, 91–93, 94
    Outcome-Item Reference Map, 27–30, 31
mastery quizzes, 27, 28
McCoy, Brenda, 6
measurement, 51–55. See also assessment; outcome
    attainment values
    census approach to, 1, 87–88
    critical thinking, 58, 65–66
    degree idea in, 10
    error, 1
    intellectual abilities and, 2
    outcome attainment, 81–82
    SLO measurability, 4, 10–12, 28
methods, test question template on procedures and, 25
Middle States Commissions on Higher Education
    (MSCHE), 85

modify, test question on change or, 24
motor skills, 2
MSCHE. See Middle States Commissions on Higher Education
multiple-choice (MC) items, 38–45. See also answer choices; selected-response (SR) items
    anatomy of, 17, 18
    answer choices, 40–43, 71–73
    averaging rubric attainment values with values of, 79
    chemistry course example of, 34
    constructed-response as, 17
    critical thinking item set with, 59–60
    for critical thinking measurement, 57–68
    developing test forms, 34–35
    directions placement, 41
    discipline-specific MC item set, 63–64
    item-analysis report for, 71
    item format guidelines, 43–44
    outcome-based model for, 37–38
    possible test questions, 61
    quality assurance checklist, 44
    question writing, 41
    short written response converted into, 62
    test blueprint with, 32–33
    two-column item-writing checklist, 45
    vignette with, 62–63
    written-response vs., 60–62

National Institute for Learning Outcomes Assessment (NILOA), 86
none of the above, 42

one-page format, 37, 38, 39
opinion, test question template on fact vs., 23
ORM. See Outcome-Item Reference Map
outcome attainment
    different disciplines, 93
    institutional level calculation of, 90
    program level, 88–89
    reporting with criterion, 82–83
outcome attainment values, 69, 73–81, 90–91
    critical thinking with equal weighting, 80
    mapping, 85
    Outcome Attainment Calculator, 5
    spreadsheet, 76, 76
    written-response rubric scores, 78–79
outcome-based assessment, 2
    model, 37–38, 81–82
Outcome-Item Reference Map (ORM), 27–30, 31
outcome statements. See also student learning outcomes; specific learning outcome level
    for AA&U LEAP critical thinking VALUE rubric, 68

aids for writing, 40
critical-thinking, 13–16
definition and purpose of, 2
guidelines for writing, 10–12
hierarchical model use for, 11
Outcome Statement Builder, 5
proper way or procedure intent, 18
questions for writing, 12
reference maps for, 10–11
student behavior expectations and, 11
task difficulty and, 12
taxonomy use in, 12
templates, 17–26
Overall Assessment Plan
    chart of test types and total points, 28
    developing, 27–35

passage. See prompts
perceptual skills, 2
performance-based assessment, 49–50, 59–60
position, test question template on, 24
position paper, 53
prediction, test question template on, 24–25
principle, test question on, 25
problem solving, 15
procedures, test question template on, 25
proficiency descriptors, analytic rubric with, 51–54
program level, 88–89
    linking goals, 84, 90
prompts, 48–49, 60, 63, 67
proper way
    procedure or, 18
    test question using correct or, 22
psychomotor domain, 2

qualifiers, for test question difficulty, 19–20
quality assurance checklist
    for multiple-choice items, 44
    for outcome statements, 13
questions. See also test questions
    for writing outcome statements, 12

random guessing, 43
rationale, test questions using reason and, 25
reaction, response, test questions using, 25
recall/factual/literal category, 47
recall knowledge category, 7–8
    Bloom's taxonomy and, 34
recognize and identify, 19, 33, 34
recommendations
    critical thinking and, 16
    test questions using suggestions and, 26

reference maps, for outcome statements, 10–11. See also
Outcome-Item Reference Map
relationships, test questions using, 26
reporting, three-level model, 69–84
    item-analysis, 71
    outcome attainment, 82–83
    outcome attainment with criterion, 82–83
    summary, 77–78
response, test questions using reaction and, 25
restricted written-response items, 48
Rhodes, T. L., 87
rubrics
    analytic, 51–54
    attainment for written-response, 78–79
    averaging attainment values with MC values, 79
    for constructed-response items, 51–55
    holistic, 51, 52
    mapping with AAC&U, 92–93
    student prior knowledge of, 52
    three-level model conversion of, 66
    writing guidelines, 54–55

SACSCOC. See Southern Association of Colleges and
    Schools Commission on Colleges
scoring, 22, 52, 57. See also rubrics
    errors in, 40
    weighted, 53–54, 80, 81
selected-response (SR) items, 2, 13, 17, 18
    test blueprint with constructed-response items and,
    31–33
sentence-completion items, 47
short-answer items, 47–48
short responses, 27–28, 62
skills category, 1–2
sLO. See specific learning outcome level
SLO model
    automated procedures of, 5
    general learning outcome level, 5
    Goal level, 4–5
    overview, 3–4
    practical examples of, 6–9
    specific learning outcome level, 5
    structure of, 5–6
SLOs. See student learning outcomes
sLO statements, difficulty designations for, 27–28
sociology, ORM example for, 29–30
sociology course, SLO example for, 8
Southern Association of Colleges and Schools Commission
    on Colleges (SACSCOC), 85
specific learning outcome level (sLO), 5
    attainment report with criterion at, 83
    calculating outcome attainment, 75

concurrent development of test items and, 30–31
constructed-response items and, 47
Outcome-Item-Reference Map for, 27–30, 31
test items written according to, 28
verbs in GLOs and, 10
SR. See selected-response
statements, from textbooks, 47
stem, multiple choice item, 41, 42, 45
stimulus. See prompts
student behavior expectations, 11, 28
student learning outcomes (SLOs). See also outcome
    statements; SLO model
    annotated example, 6
    assessment and, 2
    cognitive categories in construction of, 7–8
    developing, 3–16
    guidelines for writing measurable, 10–12
    higher level thinking, 12–13
    matching performance-based assessments to, 49
    measurability, 4, 10–12, 28
    primary domains, 1–2
    test items matching, 38, 40
    written-response items and, 48
students
    rubrics shown to, 52
    test answer input from, 35
summary reports, 77–78
survey items, test blueprint with, 32–33
synthesis, cognitive category, 9

Taxonomy of Educational Objectives (Bloom), 7, 12, 32,
    34–35
templates. See test question templates
test blueprint, 28, 30, 33, 35
    goal-verb specific, 32, 34
    scenarios, 31
test forms, multiple-choice, 34–35
test items. See also answer choices, multiple-choice;
    constructed-response; multiple-choice
    analysis, 21, 70–73
    clues in, 41, 42, 47, 48
    cognitive difficulty of, 12, 19–20, 27, 31, 34, 39
    concurrent development of outcomes and, 30–31
    continuous improvement process for, 37
    field testing, 35
    flawed, 35
    instructions, 17, 24, 25, 39, 50
    item-to-outcome statement relationship, 38, 40
    number of, 28
    one-page format, 37, 38, 39
    parts of, 17
    revising, 35

selected-response, 2, 13, 17, 18, 31–33
   terminology, 40–41
   trying out, 34–35
   types of, 2
   validity, 70
   writing drafts of, 34
   written according to sLO, 28
test questions
   avoiding broad, 49
   examples and comparisons, 61
   increasing cognitive difficulty of, 19–20
   trick, 41
   writing multiple-choice, 41
test question templates, 17–26
   classification in, 21–22
   on conflict, 25
   on events, 23
   explaining, 23
   list of, 20–26
   modify instruction in, 24
   option use in, 24
   on parts, elements and features, 24
   preparation instruction in, 25
   on problem and conflict, 25
   for procedures and rules, 25
   on purpose and main idea, 25
   on use of examples, 23
tests
   critical thinking measurement, 58
   developing multiple-choice, 34–35
   final cumulative exam, 27
   mastery quizzes, 27, 28
   products for online, 95
   score reliability in, 22

student input on answers, 35
   total points for various types of, 28
textbook statements, 47
think critically, as cognitive category, 10
thinking. See also critical thinking
   types of, 12
three-level model, 85–95
   multiple-choice conversion into, 66
   with outcome attainment values, 90–91
   overview, 88
   reporting results with, 69–84
topic planning guide, 3–5, 37
traffic accident, 65–66, 67
trick questions, 41
true-false formats, 43
Tuning USA, 86, 89, 92, 93

understand, multiple-choice items on, 34
Using the VALUE Rubrics for Improvement of Learning
   and Authentic Assessment (Rhodes/Finley), 87

Valid Assessment of Learning in Undergraduate Education
   (VALUE), 1, 68, 87, 89
validity evidence, 2, 34, 70, 89
VALUE. See Valid Assessment of Learning in
   Undergraduate Education
verbs, 10, 11, 32, 34

web tools, SLO automated procedures, 5
weighted scoring, 53–54, 80, 81
Western Governors University (WGU), 86
written-response items, 48–49, 57
   multiple-choice items vs., 60–62
   rubric scores and attainment calculation, 78–79

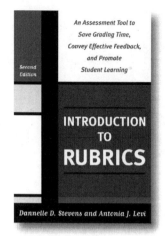